Exploration in the World of the Middle Ages, 500–1500

Revised Edition

DISCOVERY & EXPLORATION

Exploration in the World of the Middle Ages, 500–1500
Revised Edition

PAMELA WHITE

JOHN S. BOWMAN and MAURICE ISSERMAN
General Editors

CHELSEA HOUSE
PUBLISHERS
An imprint of Infobase Publishing

*The author would like to acknowledge
the contributions of Harry Anderson and Tom Smith—
for Chapter 9 and Chapter 5, respectively.*

Exploration in the World of the Middle Ages, 500–1500, Revised Edition
Copyright © 2010 by Infobase Publishing

Chelsea House
An imprint of Infobase Publishing
132 West 31st Street
New York, NY 10001

Library of Congress Cataloging-in-Publication Data
White. Pamela.
 Exploration in the world of the middle ages, 500-1500 / Pamela White, John S. Bowman, and Maurice Isserman, general editors. -- Rev. ed.
     p. cm. -- (Discovery and exploration)
 Includes bibliographical references and index.
 ISBN 978-1-60413-193-2 (hardcover)
 1. Discoveries in geography--History--To 1500. I. White, Pamela II. Bowman, John Stewart, 1931- III. Isserman, Maurice. IV. Title. V. Series.
 G82.W45 2010
 910.9'02--dc22

                                    2009030202

Chelsea House books are available at special discounts when purchased in bulk quantities for businesses, associations, institutions, or sales promotions. Please call our Special Sales Department in New York at (212) 967-8800 or (800) 322-8755.

You can find Chelsea House on the World Wide Web at
http://www.chelseahouse.com

Text design by Erika Arroyo
Cover design by Keith Trego
Composition by EJB Publishing Services
Cover printed by Bang Printing, Brainerd, MN
Book printed and bound by Bang Printing, Brainerd, MN
Date printed: December 2009
Printed in the United States of America

10 9 8 7 6 5 4 3 2 1

This book is printed on acid-free paper.

All links and Web addresses were checked and verified to be correct at the time of publication. Because of the dynamic nature of the Web, some addresses and links may have changed since publication and may no longer be valid.

Contents

1

The Grand Fleet of Treasure Ships

ON JUNE 29, 1430, THE EMPEROR OF CHINA, XUANDE (HSÜAN-TE), sent an order to his admiral Zheng He (Cheng Ho):

> *I have received Heaven's mandate and I have inherited a great empire. . . . [But] distant lands beyond the seas have not yet been informed. I send . . . Zheng He . . . to instruct these countries to follow the way of Heaven with reverence and to watch over their people so that all might enjoy the good fortune of lasting peace.*

Zheng had been assigned as a boy to the service of Zhu Di, a northern Chinese prince. Zheng had risen over the years to become a trusted general. When Zhu Di was enthroned as the emperor Yongle (Yung-lo) in 1402, he gave Zheng an important job. He ordered Zheng to "take general command of the treasure ships and go to the various foreign countries in the Western Ocean to read out the imperial commands and to bestow rewards." Zheng led six expeditions to kingdoms from the East Indies to Africa. His fleets were the largest and most powerful the world had ever seen.

In 1430, eight years after his sixth expedition, the veteran admiral received his final commission from Yongle's grandson, Xuande. Once again Zheng assembled his fleet. It was made up of 100 enormous ships bearing names such as *Pure Harmony* and *Lasting Tranquility*. The 27,500 officers and crew included seamen, soldiers, scholars, scientists, secretaries, interpreters, artisans, astrologers, and meteorologists.

The plan was, even for Zheng, ambitious. His ships sailed from Nanjing on January 19, 1431. By the time they returned in the summer of 1433 they had visited Champa (present-day Vietnam), Java, Sumatra, Malacca, Ceylon (Sri Lanka), and the Indian seaport of Calicut. Part of the fleet had sailed to the great Persian Gulf port of Hormuz and the Arabian ports of Dhofar, Aden, and Jidda. The other part of the fleet had crossed the Indian Ocean to East Africa. These ships visited the trading stations of Mogadishu and Brava (both in present-day Somalia) and of Malindi (Kenya). Zheng's fleet had sailed an amazing 12,600 miles (20,277 kilometers), sometimes covering more than 100 miles (160.9 km) a day. Although no definite evidence exists, recent scholarship suggests that Zheng probably died in India on the return voyage. Nevertheless, he became a national hero in China and the subject of novels and plays.

CHINA'S IMPERIAL POLICIES

Chinese navigators and traders had worked in the South China Sea and the Indian Ocean for 1,000 years. The policy of Zheng's original patron, the Yongle emperor, was one of close control. Yongle fine-tuned China's unique system of tributary trade, under which the goods brought to China by foreign merchants and ambassadors were given to the emperor as gifts. The foreigners were rewarded with Chinese luxury goods of at least equal value, chiefly silks, porcelain, and horses. The emperor also sent officials to foreign rulers with gifts. In return, the rulers sent more tribute back to China. Carrying these ambassadors and luxury goods to and from China was central to Zheng He's mission.

Already centuries ahead of its rivals technologically, Zheng's expedition was an achievement that made China the dominant power in the kingdoms bordering the China Sea and Indian Ocean. Still, after the triumphant conclusion of the voyage, Emperor Xuande suddenly turned his back on the outside world. He broke up the imperial fleet, destroying some vessels and reassigning others to river service. In about 1480, a

(opposite page) About half a century before the explorations of Christopher Columbus and Ferdinand Magellan, China's Zheng He made seven historical voyages to promote his country's wealth and power. The seventh voyage of the Treasure Fleet would travel 12,600 miles (20,277 km), sometimes covering more than 100 miles (160.9 km) a day.

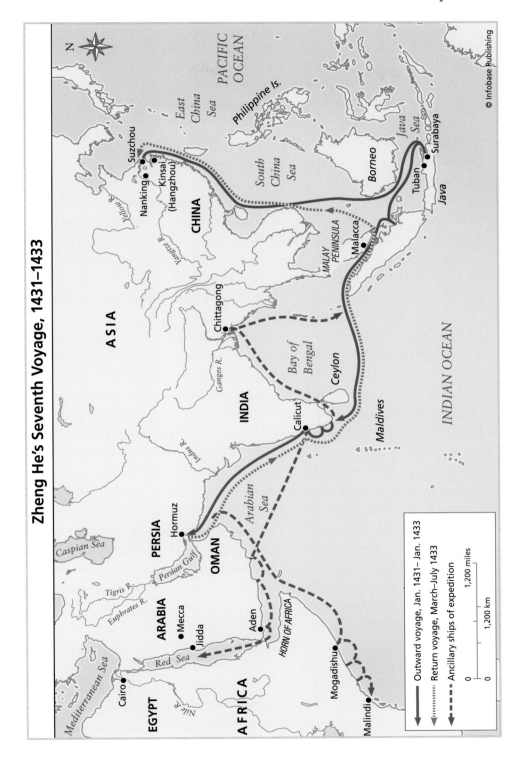

Zheng He's Seventh Voyage, 1431–1433

court official who wished to retrace Zheng's routes found that the official records of all seven expeditions had been destroyed. By 1500, it was a capital offense in China to build an oceangoing vessel with more than two masts, and in 1525, all such ships were ordered to be destroyed. The great age of Chinese maritime exploration was over.

CHINA'S NAVAL TECHNOLOGY

In the early fifteenth century, China's navy was the best in the world. Between 1404 and 1431, 2,000 ships were built for the imperial fleet. They included dozens of specialized craft: patrol and combat vessels; warships powered by rowers; water tankers containing enough freshwater to supply the thousands-strong crews for a month; supply ships carrying food for the crews and materials for repairs; transports designed to carry horses or troops.

The mainstay of the fleet, however, was the strong, oceangoing junk. These high-prowed vessels, first built in China in the eleventh century, were clinker-built. This means their outer surface consisted of overlapped wooden planks fastened with iron nails. Some were 440 feet (134 meters) long and 185 feet (56.3 m) across. They contained several decks below the main deck and three more above it at the stern. The largest war junks carried 450–700 crew members. Chinese junks from this time remain some of the largest wooden ships ever built.

Junks were able to cut through heavy seas because they had a very deep, sharp keel (structure in the bottom that provides stability). They had internal watertight compartments, which were not used in Europe for nearly 400 years. Another innovation was the junk's huge rudder (a vertical blade that helps the ship turn direction while in motion). Junks had from one to nine masts staggered across the deck. The masts carried sails made of canvas or matting. Complex rigging was designed for maximum flexibility. These features made junks very responsive and maneuverable.

The largest of Zheng's junks were called treasure ships. They carried precious cargo. The grandest were built for display and luxury. They were intricately carved and painted, with sails made of silk.

For all their remarkable speed, strength, and range, Zheng's fleets largely followed familiar coastal routes. They never entered unknown waters. Chinese navigators used traditional navigational methods such

A junk is a large, stable ship first developed by the Chinese in the eleventh century. The largest junks ever built were those of Zheng He's. The ship's design has changed little over the centuries. This modern-day tourist junk sails in Hong Kong Harbor in Hong Kong, China.

as looking for coastal landmarks and taking depth soundings. Dead reckoning was used on familiar routes. This was a simple method of following a given direction for a specified time. The sailors understood winds, currents, and tides. They paid attention to the seasonal pattern of the monsoons.

Zheng also used some technology unavailable in Europe. The Chinese had invented the compass 1,000 years earlier. By the thirteenth century, their ships were carrying magnetic marine compasses that enabled them to steer and record precise courses. One thirteenth-century Chinese geographer noted that compasses needed to be watched closely in the open sea. He warned that lives could "depend on the slightest fraction of error." Zheng and his captains also tracked time. They burned measured sticks of incense. They also used clocks—another Chinese invention—in which the movement of sand drove the mechanism.

The Chinese had invented printing by the eighth century. Among the numerous geographical works available to Zheng were printed atlases, maps, and sea charts. He carried portolans, or coastal charts, as well as a 21-foot-long (6.4-meters-long) sailing chart of the Indian Ocean. Many of his maps showed compass directions of major routes and distances measured in watches, or shifts, of about two and a half hours. Fifteenth-century Chinese astronomy was the most advanced in the world. Sailors also had star maps for major long-distance routes. They calculated their latitude by aligning a measuring board with the horizon and using their arms to indicate the position of Polaris or the Southern Cross.

ZHENG'S SEVERAL VOYAGES

Records of Zheng's voyages are incomplete. It is known that he made a total of seven voyages between 1405 and 1433. Each trip lasted about two years. He had more than 300 ships, with a crew of 28,000. Some expeditions employed them all. Most involved at a minimum his 63 large junks.

Trade and diplomacy were his major duties, and his routes were concentrated on strategically located kingdoms and ports. The basic route Zheng followed on his first expedition (1405–1407) was the core of all his later voyages: Champa (Vietnam), Java (home to wealthy colonies of Chinese traders), Sumatra, and Malacca (an Islamic state that controlled the strategically vital Strait of Malaya). Then he took a direct run from the East Indies to Calicut, on the southwest coast of India and the most important trading center of the Indian Ocean, and on to Ceylon (present-day Sri Lanka).

On the emperor's behalf, Zheng created kingdoms and legitimized kings. He drew the East Indies, Malacca, Calicut, and other important kingdoms into China's tributary sphere. On a very few occasions, Zheng used warfare. On his first expedition he defeated the China Sea pirates. In one battle he destroyed an entire pirate fleet and killed 5,000 men. On Zheng's third voyage (1409–1411), King Alagonakkara of Ceylon attacked the Treasure Fleet with 50,000 soldiers. The admiral outwitted the king, defeating him with only 2,000 troops. Zheng's Chinese troops also suppressed a rebellion in Sumatra on his fourth expedition (1413–1415).

HOW FAR DID ZHENG HE GO?

Of all Zheng He's expeditions, his voyages along the southeast coast of Africa were the only examples of pure exploration. The Chinese certainly understood African geography much earlier than Europeans did. In 1320, the geographer Zhu Siben created the earliest map showing Africa as a southward-pointing triangle. It also showed the Zanzibar, the Blue Nile, and the Congo rivers. Some writers believe that Zheng's ships may have been the first ever to round the Cape of Good Hope.

Others believe that Zheng's ships reached Australia. The Australian evidence consists of a Chinese statue, quite possibly from the Ming dynasty (1368–1644). It was found buried in northern Australia. Aboriginal Australian legend tells of visits by a technologically advanced, golden-skinned people they called the Baijini. Zheng's interpreter Fei Xin reported that the Treasure Fleet reached Timor (present-day Indonesia), only 400 miles (643.7 km) from the northern Australian coast. Zheng's navigators could certainly have mastered the Timor Sea. However, the golden-skinned people might also have been Indonesian fishermen.

The most significant achievement of the fourth expedition, however, was to reach the ports of the Persian Gulf and East Africa. Zheng returned to the imperial court with ambassadors from 30 foreign states. In 1416, the Yongle emperor announced that the "seas had been conquered and there was quiet in the four corners." But the emperor, Zheng's longtime patron, died in 1424. It would be seven more years before Zheng undertook his seventh and greatest voyage.

THE IMPACT OF ZHENG'S VOYAGES

Zheng's expeditions were a huge success. On an inscribed stone tablet he erected on the coast of modern-day Fujian Province in China, Zheng himself declared that he had succeeded "in unifying seas and continents. . . . The countries beyond the horizon from the ends of the earth have all become subjects . . . bearing precious objects and presents" to the emperor. He had in fact extended the Chinese sphere of influence across Southeast Asia and Arabia to East Africa. This feat was all the more remarkable as it was accomplished by almost entirely peaceful means. While he commanded a powerful naval force, Zheng came as an ambassador and trader, not a conqueror.

The treasure ships allowed China to dominate trade for thousands of miles. A huge quantity of luxury goods and spices flowed into China. The emperor particularly enjoyed foreign rulers' gifts of lions, leopards, giraffes, ostriches, and other exotic animals. Foreign demand for Chinese silk, porcelain, and lacquerware increased dramatically. Chinese colonists followed in the wake of the Treasure Fleet and remained dominant in Southeast Asia until the nineteenth century.

The Treasure Fleet's voyages provided information about the Asian seas and the countries that bordered them. On the Fujian tablet, Zheng expressed satisfaction that "the distances and routes" he had traveled "may be calculated." His interpreters wrote descriptions of the geography, climate, flora and fauna, peoples, customs, products, and exports of the countries they visited.

WHY THE CHINESE WITHDREW FROM EXPLORATION

Zheng He's expeditions were among the greatest achievements in medieval exploration. The scale of his voyages were unprecedented. In 1433, China was the richest civilization in the world. It was the major global sea power. So, why did the Chinese later give it all up?

This question cannot be fully answered from the surviving documentation. China was under constant threat of attack from the Mongols to the north. Decades-long military expeditions against both the Mongols and the Vietnamese and the rebuilding of the defensive Great Wall had seriously depleted the Ming dynasty treasury. The construction of the Forbidden City in Beijing and Zheng's large naval expeditions had been costly as well. The Chinese had no interest in Europe or European products, which were inferior to their own goods. Therefore, they saw no need to seek Mediterranean or Atlantic trade routes. Finally, Emperor Xuande was swayed by advisers who promoted isolationism.

They believed agriculture, rather than trade, was the true source of imperial wealth.

In the mid-fifteenth century, Asian trade was taken over by Arab and Indian merchants. The Indian Ocean trade routes soon attracted European powers. The wealth they offered was irresistible to the people who would soon set out to explore the lands along these routes.

2

The Dark Ages or the Middle Ages?

WHAT WERE THE DARK AGES? THE TERM SUGGESTS IGNORANCE, backwardness, and superstition. For many years, it was the common name used for the period in Europe between about A.D. 475 and 800. This era came after the end of the Roman Empire (and with it the culture of classical Greece and Rome) and before the start of a Christian culture in Europe. Sometimes it was also very broadly used to describe the period from about A.D. 500 to 1000, when near-constant warfare and economic decline plagued Europe. Today, historians use the more neutral term *early Middle Ages.*

Recent historical research has uncovered evidence showing that this was in fact a time of growth in Europe. Civilization had not died. Community life continued, and scholarship was carried out in the many monasteries. Artists created objects of beauty. Trade links throughout Europe, the Mediterranean, and the Middle East were maintained. Christian pilgrims to Jerusalem were making contacts with the lands to their east.

A WORLD PERSPECTIVE

Many non-European cultures flourished during this time. In A.D. 500, about 300 to 500 million people lived on Earth. Their settlements were found in Europe, Asia, Africa, the Americas, Australia, Japan, and many islands of the Indian Ocean and the South Pacific. Only New Zealand, Iceland, and perhaps Greenland were uninhabited.

The majority of the world's people were farmers, hunter-gatherers, or nomads. They were uneducated and illiterate. Most never traveled far from home. With few exceptions, they lived in small groups or villages. Their contacts were limited to family members, neighbors, and passing travelers. Any ideas, inventions, or practical innovations that were developed tended to stay limited to a small area. News passed by word of mouth, a slow and random process over long distances.

At the same time, civilizations were flourishing that were at least as old and sometimes older than Europe's. They were found in the Middle East, India, China, and Central America. These were societies with traditions of scholarship, mathematics, astronomy, engineering, medicine, philosophy, literature, art, and transportation. They had links to neighboring peoples. The world of the early Middle Ages, then, might be thought of as a patchwork of cultures. Their primary contacts were

The Maya, a highly developed culture that peaked between A.D. 300 and 900, settled primarily in the area of the present-day Yucatán Peninsula and northern Central America. They were known for their grand architecture. One of the sites they settled was Chichén Itzá, the location of this large stone Chacmool statue. The statue, near the Temple of the Warriors, reclines and holds a flat platform for sacrifices on its lap.

with their immediate neighbors. Their direct knowledge of the world extended barely any farther. A small number of soldiers, traders, pilgrims, and missionaries did make long-distance journeys. These were the groups that were to broaden contacts and extend people's knowledge of the world in the years ahead.

CHINA IN THE EARLY MIDDLE AGES

At the beginning of the Middle Ages, the Chinese had the most advanced civilization and the highest standard of living in the world. A vast country with enormous natural resources, it had long been a rich empire governed by a strong central bureaucracy. To control such a large territory, sophisticated transportation and communication systems were needed.

Three factors primarily contributed to China's sophistication. First, China had a nearly 1,000-year-old tradition of Confucian philosophy and ethics. Scholarship and learning were important. The Chinese had access to centuries of accumulated knowledge. In astronomy, mathematics, medicine, and other sciences, China was far in advance of other cultures.

Second, China had contacts with many other cultures in Asia, India, the Middle East, and the Mediterranean. The fabulously rich city of Chang'an, the Chinese capital and the largest city on Earth at the time, was home to people from nearly every part of the known world. Many foreigners, especially Arabs, made their way to other Chinese cities as well.

Finally, the Chinese had a genius for invention. By A.D. 500, the Chinese had already invented paper, the magnetic compass, and the clock. They soon discovered printing. This inventiveness extended to the development of shipbuilding and navigational skill. China's massive mountain systems and extensive deserts made its long coastline and great river systems the easiest means of transportation.

China's geography was recorded on surveys and maps. In fact, China was fully mapped in A.D. 267. This information was used to plan roads and canals. A network of roads and water routes, post stations, and accommodations for traders and travelers connected every part of the empire.

Several overland routes reached westward from eastern China. They connected China to central Asia, Afghanistan, India, Persia, and Syria. The fabled Silk Roads, with their legendary cities and oases, luxury trade, and rich cultural exchanges, had been used by traders' caravans for hundreds of years. The well-traveled northern route ran along the Huang He (Yellow River) and crossed the Gobi and Taklimakan deserts, then headed southward through Turkestan and the high mountain passes of the Hindu Kush into present-day Pakistan. The southern overland route was even more challenging. It crossed the Himalayas through Tibet and Nepal into India.

Traveling these routes was slow and expensive. The land was rough. Thieves and the political instability of central Asian tribes often made it dangerous, even in the relative safety of caravans. Still, Buddhist missionaries and Arab, Jewish, Persian, and Turkish merchants made the journey. Chinese overland trade with India and the Mediterranean flourished during the Tang dynasty (A.D. 618–907), until political turmoil among the tribes of central Asia made travel too risky.

Chinese sailors had mastered the China Sea and the coasts of East Asia and Southeast Asia by A.D. 500. Foreign traders sailed regularly between China and the Malay Peninsula, Ceylon (present-day Sri Lanka), and India. By the seventh century, Persian and Arab sailors were trading in China. The route from the Persian Gulf to the Chinese port of Guangzhou was the longest regularly traveled sea route anywhere until the sixteenth century. The Chinese sailors never sailed far into the Pacific and had little contact with Japan. (Early medieval Japanese ships were fragile, therefore, the Japanese knew no foreign lands beyond China and Korea.)

At the same time, China faced many problems. Tribal unrest in central Asia made westward overland travel dangerous. Only foreigners were permitted to engage in foreign trade, so it was Arab and Indian sailors, not Chinese, who developed their maritime technology on the long-distance sea routes. The Chinese Empire fell apart after the fall of the Tang dynasty in A.D. 907. It was not reunified until the Mongol conquest of the thirteenth century. It was only then that China briefly opened up to the rest of the world.

The Chinese mainly looked inward. They were intellectually and technologically self-sufficient. They showed no interest in importing and studying the works of the Phoenicians, Greeks, and Romans. Nor did they seek territorial expansion. They believed that the rest of the world had little to offer them.

INDIA IN THE EARLY MIDDLE AGES

Another ancient and sophisticated Asian civilization was that of India. India, too, has many natural resources. Bordered to the north by the Himalayas, it has an extremely long coastline. By A.D. 500, Indian sailors were making good use of their access to the seas. The monsoon winds and currents of the Indian Ocean made for easy sailing.

India had a long tradition of science and advanced learning based on the Vedas, the ancient founding texts of Hinduism. Indian scholars led the world in astronomy and mathematics. Aryabhata the Elder was using the decimal system in about A.D. 500. By 550, Varahamihira had discovered zero. By the sixth century, Indian mathematicians had also created the symbols that are misleadingly called "Arabic" numerals. These advances gave Indian sailors the tools to navigate in open seas 1,000 years before European sailors. By the early medieval period, India had long-established trade links throughout the Indian Ocean region. Sea routes connected India to Arabia, the Persian Gulf, Java, and Sumatra.

India also had overland routes to central Asia and the Middle East. These routes were slower than the sea-lanes, but they were still popular. Buddhist missionaries from India reached China in the fourth century. They converted many Chinese from Daoism and Confucianism. The Chinese emperor banned Buddhism in the ninth century. By then, Buddhism had spread to the East Indies. A shared religion strengthened the trade links of this region with India.

Like China, India in the sixth century seemed ready to explore the wider world. But India, too, was subject to restraining factors. South Asia was divided into many kingdoms engaged in constant warfare. No single kingdom controlled politics, communications, or trade. None were interested in conquering distant territories.

India's people were not interested in exploration. Buddhism was a quiet, contemplative faith. Another native belief system, Hinduism, had intellectual traditions. Its reach never extended much beyond India. The ancient texts of India were written in Sanskrit, a language unknown outside of South Asia. Fortunately, the knowledge of Indian scholars, shipbuilders, and sailors was passed on to Arabs. The Arab traders were eager to learn from Indian sailors and master the Indian Ocean and reach the East Indies themselves.

ARABS AND ISLAM IN THE EARLY MIDDLE AGES

In A.D. 500, the Middle East was politically disorganized, but this was about to change. The prophet Muhammad founded Islam by the early seventh century, and the religion spread rapidly. In less than a century it united Arab peoples across a vast region, from the western Mediterranean to northwestern India. People in these lands came together under a single faith. They shared a culture and a common language, Arabic. They also shared economic and political systems. The caliphs, or Islamic rulers, followed the lead of the Roman emperors. They built a network of roads for messengers and armies. These roads linked distant regions.

The development of a specifically Islamic culture was promoted with the requirement that every Muslim make one pilgrimage to Mecca, in western Arabia, during his or her lifetime. This yearly pilgrimage, called the hajj, brought together people from a huge geographical area. They returned home to spread information about the lands through which they had traveled. Muslims became the greatest travelers of the Middle Ages.

In the early Middle Ages, Muslim scholars were unique in having the benefit of ancient Greek, Roman, Persian, and Indian texts, which they translated into Arabic. In addition to science, philosophy, and medicine, they excelled at astronomy and mathematics. They translated Ptolemy's the *Almagest* and *Geography.* These books contained a great deal of astronomical and geographical information. Arab scholars also translated the astronomical and mathematical work *Brahmasiddhanta*, written by the seventh-century Indian astronomer Brahmagupta. In comparison, Ptolemy's works were unavailable to Europeans until translators converted the text from Greek to Latin in the fifteenth century.

Muslim traders added to geographical knowledge. Muhammad himself had been a merchant, and Islamic societies held trade in high esteem. The combination of sea and overland routes put Muslims in communication with much of the known world. Experienced Egyptian and Persian shipbuilders built fleets for Muslim traders. Muslim navigators learned from and improved on Indian, Arab, and Persian sailors familiar with the Indian Ocean.

Geography and astronomy were important areas of study because Muslim traders and Bedouin land caravans used the stars to navigate. In addition, in observance of the annual pilgrimage, the hajj, people came together from many different areas and shared information. Pictured is a page of Islamic text from the seventeenth century depicting the universe.

Basra, in present-day Iraq, was founded in A.D. 638. It quickly became the most important seaport in the Persian Gulf. Muslim merchants were in India by the mid-eighth century and soon built their own communities along India's western coast. Detailed written instructions for sailing in the Indian Ocean were recorded by Arab and Persian sailors in the eighth century. By the ninth century, Middle Eastern traders were settling in the East Indies.

The Islamic holy book, the Qur'an (Koran), describes the world as two seas, the Mediterranean Sea and the Indian Ocean. It states that these seas are separated by an overwhelming barrier. But Muslims valued experience and evidence as well as the Qur'an's spiritual authority, and the discoveries of generations of pilgrims, merchants, and other travelers were welcomed. Islamic geographers gathered and passed on huge amounts of accurate information.

Their knowledge of Islamic regions was detailed and precise. The more distant from their homelands, however, the less reliable their information became. Islamic geographers knew very little about northern Europe or East Asia. Their trust in Ptolemy led them to believe that the Indian Ocean was an inland sea and that the landmasses were larger than they really are. Like the other inhabitants of the Eastern Hemisphere, they had no idea of the existence of the Americas.

Nevertheless, the Islamic world benefited from sophisticated geographical information. The Islamic empires were centrally located, sharing borders with Europe, Africa, and Asia. Their focus, however, was confined to Islamic territories, and their discoveries did not spread among neighboring, non-Arabic-speaking cultures.

EUROPE IN THE EARLY MIDDLE AGES

By almost every measure, Europe lagged significantly behind the Chinese, Indians, and Arabs in A.D. 500. Europe was relatively poor in resources. Its Roman roads and waterworks were decaying. Its people were poor. The Roman Empire had collapsed, and the small kingdoms and principalities that succeeded the Roman Empire were weak. They were repeatedly attacked by the Germanic tribes from the north.

The only stable force among western Europeans during the early medieval period was the Christian church. Ireland, Gaul (modern-day France), and Britain had all been Christianized by the sixth century.

In the absence of strong political structures, the most powerful central authority was the highest church official: the pope. He ran a new kind of church-state: Christendom. Monasteries were the sole custodians of ancient Greek and Roman learning. Monks became the Europeans' only source of written geographical information. Almost all of it came from Roman sources. They knew little about Africa beyond its Mediterranean coastline or of Asia beyond the Near East.

Most Christian scholarship was not based on factual evidence. Instead of correcting their sources by means of direct observations or measurements, geographers developed cosmographies, or descriptions that agreed with the Bible. The Bible was viewed as the sole source of truth. Firsthand experience was beside the point—with one exception. Personal visits to the Holy Land were felt to intensify religious faith.

EARLY MEDIEVAL TRAVEL

Travel in the early Middle Ages was slow, difficult, expensive, and dangerous. The 3,000-mile (4,828-km) network of old Roman roads in Europe needed repair and lacked sign posts. The roads often dwindled into tracks. Some ended at bridgeless rivers. Travelers between northern and southern Europe had to cross the Alps using several major routes through high mountain passes. Weather was their biggest problem. Brother John of Canterbury, an English monk, described his misery crossing the Alps in 1188: "I found my ink bottle filled with a dry mass of ice. My fingers refused to write; my beard was stiff with frost, and my breath congealed in a long icicle. I could not write."

Only the rich or noble rode on horseback, and clerics rode on mules. The rest went on foot. European pilgrims to Jerusalem faced a 3,000-mile trek, and some of them walked barefoot. If traveling by sea, the rich enjoyed comfortable, leisurely passages by hiring private vessels that offered a high standard of food and accommodation and took safe coastal routes. Others took passage on small cargo ships, huddling together on the open decks or hunched in cramped, stinking accommodations below deck. Sea voyages

The most important early medieval geographical text in Europe was the *Etymologiae* (Etymologies, or Origins). It was written by the Spanish bishop Isidore of Seville (ca. A.D. 560–636). This work influenced explorers up to and including Christopher Columbus (1451–1506). Based largely on Ptolemy's writings, it was an encyclopedia of all the knowledge a Christian needed. The *Etymologies* located Paradise as one of the four provinces of Asia and the source of the four great rivers of the world (the Nile, Ganges, Tigris, and Euphrates). More accurately, the known world was bounded by the country of Seres (literally, the "source of silk," that is, China), the Malay Peninsula, India, Ceylon, islands off the West African coast, and the island Ultima Thule (possibly Iceland). This was roughly the world known to the Romans.

threatened danger: storms, shipwreck, pirate attacks, and the crossfire of war. Passengers also suffered from diseases and infections caused by filth, vermin, bad food, and foul water. Ships could become becalmed—unmoving due to lack of wind—for weeks at a time, until there was no food or water at all.

Long-distance travel was expensive. Apart from the cost of transportation, food, and lodging, tolls and bribes were repeatedly demanded en route. Some travelers worked odd jobs or brought goods to trade along the way, while others begged. Travelers who carried cash or valuables were extremely vulnerable, for highwaymen and bandits infested the roads.

Monasteries provided travelers with shelter, food, warmth, and fresh water. Bishops set up hostels along major routes. Usually run as charities by religious orders or monks, the hostels provided travelers with free lodging—usually on straw mats on the floor—water, and sometimes food, baths, and medical care. These accommodations were not always available, however, and many travelers were forced to sleep in the open.

Other geographical texts also influenced early medieval Europeans. The *Historiarum adversus paganos libri septem* (Seven books of history against the pagans), written by the fifth-century Spanish priest Orosius, remained influential until the thirteenth century. The book described a region from the British Isles to the Red Sea, extending southward as far as Egypt, Ethiopia, and the Nile. Orosius believed Africa to be uninhabitable and quite small. The sixth-century *De origine actibusque Getarum* (On the origin and deeds of the Getae) was written by the historian Jordanes. It focused on Scandza (Scandinavia), describing the region as a large northern island that was the homeland of the Goths.

A world map drawn in Ravenna, Italy, in the seventh century and another by the Spanish monk Beatus in the eighth century showed land as far east as India. *De mensura orbis terrae* (Concerning the measurement of the world), was written in the early ninth-century by the Irish monk Dicuil. It contained very inaccurate geographical statistics and measurements of the two seas, 72 islands, 40 mountains, 281 towns, and 55 rivers that he believed made up the world. More important, he also gave an account, based on firsthand reports, of the discovery of Iceland.

The western Europeans had the deepest and most accurate information about the geography of their own land and seas. Because the easiest, cheapest, and fastest transportation in Europe was by water, they had a variety of sturdy river and coastal ships to carry trade goods. They lacked advanced shipbuilding and navigational skills that would have allowed them to sail in open seas. They could not master the strong Atlantic currents off the Strait of Gibraltar at the western end of the Mediterranean Sea. This technological handicap took centuries to overcome.

OTHER REGIONS' VIEWS IN THE EARLY MIDDLE AGES

Africa is a huge continent whose interior is characterized by extremes of climate and terrain. Agriculture and overland communication are nearly impossible across its huge deserts and jungles. The coasts offer few natural harbors, and the currents off western and southern Africa are difficult and very dangerous to navigate.

The Aztec calendar (*above*) was used by the Aztecs as well as other pre-Columbian peoples in central Mexico. Adapted from the Mayan calendar, the Aztecs used two different calendars. One measured time (for example, the best time to plant crops), while the other was used to organize religious festivals (the best time to consult the gods). At the center was the sun god, who is surrounded by symbols.

In A.D. 500, Africa was occupied by numerous different tribes of farmers and hunter-gatherers. Most Africans knew little about territories beyond their own immediate lands. Coastal peoples used dugout canoes for short distances, hugging the shores. They had no means of long-distance travel by either land or sea. The settlements of western and southern Africa, in particular, were isolated from each other and the rest of the world.

There were a few exceptions. Camel caravans began crossing the western Sahara Desert about A.D. 300. They linked the coast and the interior. The people of northern and northeastern Africa had traded with Greece and Arabia. The kingdom of Aksum was located in present-day Ethiopia. It controlled the gold trade. Aksum was the main trading power in the Red Sea from the fourth century to the eighth century. It was conquered by Islamic armies. By that time, traders from Indonesia were visiting a handful of East African ports.

Foreign visitors to Africa were mostly merchants. Although they were familiar with the Mediterranean coast of North Africa, they had little knowledge of the east coast. They knew nothing about the huge size or the shape of the continent. Europeans would not have the ship-building and navigational capabilities required to explore Africa's long west coast for nearly a thousand years. They did not fully map the African interior until the nineteenth century.

The Pacific Ocean, meanwhile, was home to the Polynesians, who were expert sailors. By the early Middle Ages, the Polynesians had explored much of the Pacific Ocean's 70 million square miles (181 million sq km). They visited a large number of island groups, and in about A.D. 400, they settled the Hawaiian Islands and Easter Island.

The Native Americans lived in the Americas. They were hunter-gatherers, farmers, and fishermen. Most only had localized geographical knowledge. One exception was the major civilization of the Maya. The Maya reached the height of their power between about A.D. 300 and A.D. 900. They lived in modern-day Mexico, Guatemala, and Belize. Their planned cities, advanced mathematics, complex calendar, and system of writing made them one of the world's most advanced cultures at the time. They had trade and diplomatic contacts with neighboring peoples. They mapped their own lands. These maps helped them record migrations, trade, and conquests. The Maya, however, did not travel long distances. Their influence and their geographical knowledge remained purely regional.

At the start of the European Middle Ages, the people of the eastern and western hemispheres were separated by vast oceans. They knew nothing of each other. People were far from having a complete geographical understanding of the world. However, the world's merchants, missionaries, and pilgrims were beginning to explore others' lands. Quite clearly, the term *Dark Ages* does an injustice to the intelligence and vitality of the people who lived in the early Middle Ages.

3

Pilgrims and Missionaries of the Early Middle Ages

Traveling to holy places for spiritual purification is an ancient custom. The *Epic of Gilgamesh*, one of the world's oldest known stories, celebrates the journey of a hero to the underworld where the gods live. The Vedic texts, religious writings from India dating from about 1500 B.C., describe pilgrimages to sacred rivers and mountains. The ancient Greeks visited the shrines of their gods, too, at sites where they could consult oracles and, during the Olympic Games, the great temple of Zeus at Olympia. By the beginning of the Middle Ages, the practice of taking to the road to visit holy sites was several thousand years old.

Between A.D. 500 and 800, the spread of three great religions—Buddhism, Christianity, and Islam—inspired the first wave of medieval long-distance travel. Missionaries and pilgrims crisscrossed Europe and Asia. Only merchants traveled in larger numbers or covered longer distances. Many of the people traveling for religious purposes were true pioneers and pathfinders. Many of the accounts they wrote of their travels served to introduce remote and little-known parts of the world to a larger public.

BUDDHIST PILGRIMS ACROSS ASIA

Following Buddha's instructions, his ashes and other relics were divided after his death in 483 B.C. and placed in large dome-shaped shrines called stupas. These were located in northern India at eight sites the Buddha himself identified as places of pilgrimage, chief among them the locations of his birth and death and the places where he preached his first sermon and achieved enlightenment.

Spread largely by missionaries along trade routes, Buddhism rapidly established itself throughout southern and eastern Asia, from India and Ceylon through the kingdoms of Southeast Asia, Sumatra, and Java and into China. By the fifth century A.D., China had become a major center of the faith along with India, and close ties were maintained between their Buddhist communities.

For the next 300 years, a number of Chinese Buddhist travelers made their way to India. They were primarily scholars seeking to learn. They wanted to study Buddhist teachings and practice at their source. Copies of these Sanskrit texts, the ancient language of India, were carried back to China. These texts were translated into Chinese, forming the basis of the distinct schools and traditions of Chinese Buddhism.

The first known Chinese Buddhist pilgrim was Faxian. He traveled overland from eastern China to India in A.D. 399. Faxian spent 10 years in northern India before returninig home by ship. Faxian brought with him a cargo of precious Buddhist statues and texts.

Trekking the Silk Road, crossing the Himalayas, or putting out to sea, many Chinese Buddhists followed Faxian on what they called a "Western journey," seeking out the holy sites and scholars of India. Historically dominated by traders, Chinese-Indian relations were maintained by Buddhist pilgrims during the Sui and Tang dynasties (A.D. 589–907), a golden age for China. The country had not only become the world's most technologically and culturally advanced society but also the world center of Buddhism.

The most famous Chinese pilgrim was Xuanzang, a Buddhist monk who visited more than 110 countries and cities. He covered more than 16,000 miles (25,749.5 km) during a trip to India that lasted 16 years. Thanks to his written account, *Record of the Western Regions,* his pilgrimage is documented in more detail than any comparable journey of the age.

Xuanzang set out from southern China in A.D. 629. On the way, he got lost in the Gobi Desert, where he ran out of water. His only means of navigation was "by following the heaps of bones and the horse-dung. . . . In all four directions the expanse was boundless . . . in the night the

From about A.D. 400, Buddhist pilgrims from as far away as China visited holy sites in northern India. Buddhism rapidly spread along trade routes throughout southern and eastern Asia by missionaries. This statue of Buddha is in Narathiwat province in Thailand.

demons and goblins raised fire-lights to confound the stars." Xuanzang's life was saved by his horse. It led him to an oasis when he himself was stupefied by exposure, hunger, and fatigue.

After two years of spiritual preparation in Kashmir, on the present-day India-Pakistan border, Xuanzang made his way among the Buddhist temples along the Ganges River valley. He noted that "millions" of them had been sacked by marauding Huns. He studied philosophy at the great Buddhist university at Nalanda in northeastern India. He traveled the length of India's east and west coasts before returning overland on the caravan route to Chang'an, the Chinese imperial capital. Xuanzang had made a longer journey than any pilgrim ever had before.

Although Xuanzang had been denied official permission to make his trip, Xuanzang was welcomed home by the emperor Taizong. His report described the geography, culture, and politics of central Asia and India. It had enormous practical value to an emperor interested in organizing military campaigns in distant regions.

Numerous other Chinese Buddhists traveled throughout Asia. These travelers could choose from four established routes, three overland and one by sea. The emperor or others often sponsored the pilgrimages, and the travelers took goods to barter en route. They stayed in Buddhist monasteries, often carrying silk textiles and garments with which to pay their monastic hosts or to endow shrines.

The prospect of journeying thousands of miles was no obstacle to the Buddhist faithful. People commonly traveled long distances to visit the Buddha's relics in northern India. In addition, pilgrims from as far away as Tibet and India traveled to certain sacred mountains in China, the most famous being Mount Wutai in the northeast of the country.

Travel was made possible by the wealth, open-mindedness, and support of China's Tang emperors. Tang power, however, began to decline by the end of the eighth century. The western trade routes were cut off by hostile Arabs and Tibetans a century later. During his short reign in the 840s, Chinese emperor Wuzong suppressed Buddhism, destroying tens of thousands of temples and shrines. He forced more than a quarter of a million Buddhist monks and nuns to leave their religious lives. Wuzong's rule ended the great period of Chinese Buddhist pilgrimages to India.

CHRISTIAN PILGRIMS IN EUROPE AND THE MIDDLE EAST

By A.D. 500, Christianity had expanded over a very wide geographical area in western Europe and the Mediterranean. It stretched eastward into the Byzantine Empire with its capital in Constantinople. Christian missionaries spread the religion, making them great travelers.

St. Patrick and St. Augustine converted the peoples of Britain and Ireland to Christianity. Irish monks became famous as missionaries throughout northern and western Europe. They sailed out to sea in long, solitary voyages at the mercy of the weather, winds, and ocean currents. They used small boats called coracles, or curraghs. These boats were made of a light, wooden frame covered with animal hide waterproofed with tallow and fitted with sails and oars. In the course of these spiritual retreats in the far northern Atlantic Ocean, Irish monks sailing on these small ships discovered the Faeroe Islands and Iceland, where they were the first settlers in the late eighth century.

The majority of Christian travelers in the Middle Ages, however, were pilgrims. They were ordinary people who spent long periods, sometimes many years, facing financial hardship, life-threatening hazards, and the terrors of long-distance travel in order to visit holy sites. Mortality was high. Scholars estimate that during some periods, 10 percent of medieval pilgrims died on their travels. The Venerable Bede (ca. A.D. 673–735), an English historian, wrote that pilgrims hoped "to live as pilgrims on earth that they might be welcomed by the saints when they were called away from their earthly sojourn."

The pilgrims visited Christian sites in the Holy Land connected with the life and ministry of Jesus and incidents related in the Bible. The Holy Land refers to Jerusalem and the surrounding region, parts of modern-day Israel and Jordan. In speaking of the ancient region, the Holy Land is sometimes also called Palestine. Most of the early Christians came from the east, especially Mesopotamia (modern-day

(opposite page) The early Christian pilgrims journeyed to sites connected to the birth, life, crucifixion, and resurrection of Jesus. These included the core sites of the Holy Land (Jerusalem, Bethelehem, Nazareth, Golgotha). Pilgrimages also were made to sites associated with the apostles, saints, and monks.

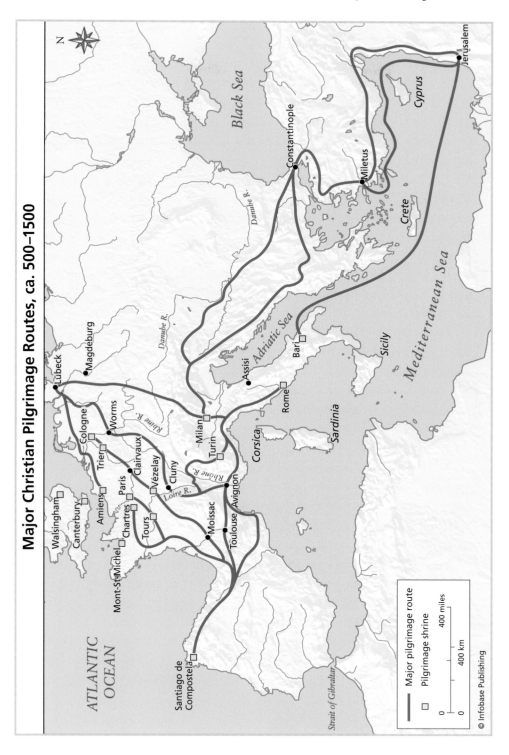

Major Christian Pilgrimage Routes, ca. 500–1500

Major pilgrimage route
□ Pilgrimage shrine

© Infobase Publishing

Iraq), where Jewish communities had long been in contact with Jews living in Jerusalem. They visited the spot in Bethlehem where Jesus was born. They climbed Golgotha (Calvary), the hill on which he was crucified. They went to the Mount of Olives, where he ascended into heaven. They also visited the Holy Sepulcher, the tomb in which he was buried. These pilgrims often extended their travels to visit apostles' tombs and saints' shrines as well as holy hermits and monks in Egypt, Syria, and Mesopotamia.

In the 320s and 330s, the Roman emperor Constantine, who had converted to Christianity, rebuilt existing sites in Jerusalem and built a magnificent new Jerusalem. It had great churches, golden and marble buildings, and public spaces. These spaces were designed for large crowds of pilgrims. The discovery in A.D. 326 by his mother, Helena, of the True Cross—allegedly the very one on which Jesus was crucified—attracted thousands of Christians. By the fifth century, there were 200 hostels for pilgrims in Jerusalem.

In the early Middle Ages, Christian pilgrims were likely to be clerics, scholars, or noblewomen. These were an educated, cultured elite whose common language was Latin, the language of Christianity. Many Christian pilgrims wrote accounts of their travels. They described the routes, sites, and relics for the benefit of other would-be pilgrims. Antoninus of Placentia made a pilgrimage from Italy in about A.D. 560–570, traveling through the Sinai Peninsula, Egypt, Syria, and Mesopotamia in addition to the Holy Land. A companion wrote an account of the trip, the *Itinerarium* (Itinerary). Some information is reliable, such as his report of the well-organized system of charitable hostels in the Holy Land. These provided shelter, food, and medical care. Antoninus estimated that in total they could accommodate 3,000 people.

As time went on, these travellers diversified and pilgrims were men and women, rich and poor, old and young. Rome, home to the tombs of the apostles St. Peter and St. Paul, was a popular pilgrimage destination, too. The seventh-century West Saxon kings Caedwalla and Ina abdicated their thrones to make pilgrimages there. The emperor Charlemagne himself made a pilgrimage to Rome in A.D. 800. His biographer, Einhard, wrote that he "spent some few days there in his personal devotions at the holy places."

A substantial "publishing" industry developed to serve the growing pilgrim population. Aside from the pilgrims' own narratives, itineraries, guides to sites and accommodations, and travel guides were popular. There were phrasebooks in European languages, Greek, and Hebrew, and interpreters and guides competed for customers at the holy sites.

Christianity left its mark on the Holy Land. Roads were improved. Bridges were built. Churches, hostels, and other buildings were constructed. All of this contributed to the economic development of Europe and the Holy Land. Larger markets stimulated the trade of Asian luxuries. These included spices, silks, jewels, and perfumes. Travel and communication became safer and more comfortable. The care of large numbers of sick and dying travelers led to advances in medical science.

The Christian church was also changed. Pilgrims gave churches, shrines, and monasteries gifts of land, gold, and other valuables. These gifts helped create the great wealth of the later medieval church. In the meantime, however, the first great wave of Christian pilgrimage ended in the ninth century. Raids by Vikings, Magyars, Arabs, and other peoples made travel from Europe too unsafe.

MUSLIM PILGRIMAGES TO ARABIA

Islam was founded in Arabia by the prophet Muhammad in the early seventh century. During his lifetime, Muhammad (ca. A.D. 570–632) united the often quarrelsome tribes of Arabia into an Islamic union. Within 20 years after his death, Muslim missionaries reached China and Islamic armies defeated the Byzantine and Persian empires. They helped spread Islam far beyond the Arabian Peninsula.

Within a century, a vast Islamic empire was established, stretching from Spain through North Africa and the Middle East all the way to India. Islam transformed the region by introducing a common religion, language, and culture, while cementing economic ties. Islam's rapid spread was the result of conversion, alliance, and conquest. The previously existing Arab trade network that reached from the Mediterranean to China speeded the process. The Islamic pilgrimage to Mecca, the hajj, brought together the diverse peoples and cultures of this huge empire.

Pre-Islamic Arabs had a long history of making annual pilgrimages to sites associated with pagan gods. In the holy months of the year, when tribal feuds were put aside in favor of communal religious interests, Arabs would travel to specific sites in Arabia. Large fairs and markets were held annually along the major routes and at the pilgrimage

THE CANTERBURY TALES

The Canterbury Tales is a classic work of medieval English literature. It is a group of tales told by a group of English pilgrims traveling on foot from London to the shrine of St. Thomas Becket in Canterbury, about 65 miles (104.6 km) away. It was written in the early 1380s by Geoffrey Chaucer, a civil servant and diplomat.

In the tales, it is April, the beginning of fair weather for travel and therefore of the pilgrimage season. Twenty-nine pilgrims meet at the Tabard Inn in Southwark, across the Thames River from London, prior to starting their journey. Harry Bailly, the innkeeper, proposes that each of them should tell stories en route, for "It makes no sense, and really it's no fun / To ride along the road dumb [quiet] as a stone." Whoever told the "most amusing and instructive" tale would win a free dinner at the Tabard.

The Canterbury pilgrims are taking part in an unbroken Christian tradition dating back more than a thousand years of visiting shrines and places of significance to the faithful. The Canterbury pilgrims include men and women, high born and humble alike. They are religious, earthy, disrespectful, self-righteous, argumentative, and jealous. Many of them wore expensive, stylish clothing. Some of the churchmen were greedy and hypocritical.

The pilgrims amused themselves and one another with bagpipes, popular tunes, and stories about romance, wickedness, and sin. All in all, the Canterbury pilgrims were enjoying a tourist romp. Chaucer claimed that this behavior had a long tradition among pilgrims:

Every man in his wise made hearty chere,
Telling his fellows of sportes and of cheer,
And of mirthes that fallen by the waye,
As custom is of pilgrims, and hath been many a day.

sites. Mecca, in the west-central part of modern-day Saudi Arabia, was the site of a religious sanctuary known as the Kaaba. Because of its origins as an oasis on ancient caravan routes between the Mediterranean and southern Arabia, East Africa, and South Asia, Mecca was also an important regional trade center. By the Middle Ages, it was the site of one of the largest commercial fairs in the world, attracting merchants from Europe, Arabia, and the Indian Ocean. These were the pagan traditions Muhammad adapted to the hajj.

The Qur'an (Koran), the sacred text of Islam, states that all adult Muslims able to undertake it are required to make a hajj once in their lifetime. Caravans of pilgrims moved toward Mecca from south Arabia and the present-day region of Yemen, Syria, and Iraq. Many others came by ship to Jidda, the port serving Mecca and the major Arabian port on the Red Sea. Groups of North African pilgrims traveled eastward to Egypt. They joined Egyptian Muslims in Cairo. From there, groups set off for Mecca every 24 hours. This final leg of the journey—from Cairo through the port of Aqaba (in modern-day Jordan), along the eastern shore of the Red Sea, and overland to Mecca—took 35 days. Central Africans traveled overland to Port Sudan on the east coast of Africa. They sailed across the Red Sea to Jidda before making their way overland to Mecca.

These journeys were dangerous. Seafarers faced piracy, storms, and shipwreck. Pilgrims on foot could easily get lost in the desert and attacked by the nomadic peoples of the Arabian, Syrian, or North African deserts. They could also be smothered in sandstorms or drowned by flash floods. Illness and accidents threatened constantly. Extremes of temperature were yet another factor.

Islamic authorities tried to make the hajj safer by maintaining forts along the major routes. They provided caravans with military escorts and paid protection money and gifts to the tribes who owned the land through which pilgrims had to pass. Along the way, members of the Muslim elite met during these journeys, and scholars often stopped at mosques to teach. Merchants did business and learned about new products, routes, customs, and languages. Yet the hajj reinforced the central values of Islam—equality before God and the community of the faithful. Muslim pilgrims, rich and poor, representing a multitude of language, ethnic, and political groups, came together on equal terms.

Pilgrims of every faith continued to travel widely throughout the Middle Ages. Pilgrimage in the early medieval period influenced the culture of European, Asian, and North African societies. Thousands of individual travelers gained firsthand knowledge of near and distant lands, peoples, and customs. The travel guides they used and their own written accounts created a large body of travel literature. These books spread knowledge about the wider world. Pilgrims were largely uninterested in mixing with people of different beliefs or in visiting sites sacred to other religions. Still, they developed a broad sense of community across political and cultural boundaries. The world was widening.

4

The Vikings

BY THE EARLY MEDIEVAL PERIOD—ABOUT A.D. 750—THE EUROPEAN continent was already well traveled. Kings and their messengers, armies, Christian priests and church officials, pilgrims, and merchants could be seen in large numbers on what remained of the old Roman roads. One European region, however, was a stark exception to this mobility: the far northern region known in the present day as Scandinavia.

Scandinavia was remote, located across the frigid North Sea and Baltic Sea from the European mainland. It was largely mountainous and cold. These lands were unknown to continental Europeans, who believed that no one lived in the frozen northern latitudes. Scandinavian peoples were further isolated by their language and by their religion. In turn, these peoples knew nothing of the geographical discoveries made in the Mediterranean, Africa, and Asia by the ancient Greeks and Romans, the Hindus, and the Arabs.

The Northmen, or Norse, as they were called, lived in modern-day Denmark, Norway, and Sweden. They shared a set of values that prized strength, courage, and military skill as the basis of a person's reputation.

Their ferocity and skill as fighters indirectly gave the Northmen their popular name—the Vikings. From the late eighth through the mid-eleventh centuries, Norse raiding parties attacked the northwestern European coast. They swooped in from the sea, looting and burning property. It is this image of vicious piracy that survived them. The name *Viking*, dating from the eighth century, derives from the word *vík*, referring either to a "creek" or "inlet"—safe moorings for their ships during raids—or to an "encampment"—their temporary base camps during invasions. In Old Norse, *víking* meant "piracy"; and the pirates were *víkingr.*

But the Vikings had another, more peaceful side. During the same period, the Swedes established an extensive trading network, reaching to the Black and Caspian seas and Constantinople (present-day Istanbul, Turkey). In an amazing feat of maritime skill, the Danes and Norse sent expeditions across the North Atlantic, settling in Iceland, Greenland, and finally North America.

Land travel was difficult in medieval Scandinavia. From the earliest of times, water provided the easiest means of communication. Centuries of fishing and trading in northern waters made the Northmen superb sailors. Early medieval Scandinavian shipbuilding, seamanship, and navigation were the finest in the world.

VIKING SHIPS

The Vikings owed their success in raiding, colonization, and trade to their advanced shipbuilding technology. By the mid-eighth century, Viking ships were powered by sails rather than oars and were stabilized by long keels. These innovations allowed them to sail across open seas at a time when other parts of Europe were largely limited to coastal sailing. It would be another 600 years before other Europeans could match the Vikings' maritime skill.

The workhorse of the Viking raiding fleets was the longship. This ship was larger, lighter, and more flexible than anything previously built. It was a long, graceful vessel whose bow and stern curved upward to end in a ferocious carved dragon's head and tail (they were sometimes called dragon boats). Its keel was an enormous single timber.

At sea, Viking longships were powered by means of a single large, square sail made of rough wool. Sails were often striped in red, green, and blue. When in shallow water or if the wind failed, the ships could also be rowed by pairs of rowers sitting on benches. They were steered with a rudder on the right-hand side of the ship as one faced front (the "steerboard," hence starboard, side). Longships ranged from 45 feet (13.7 m) to 75 feet (22.8 m) in length. They could carry three dozen people, food and water, cargo, and livestock. Warships were tarred black. Their sides were covered by the brightly painted shields of the warriors onboard.

Shown here is a replica of a Viking longship, or dragon ship. The warriors attached shields along the sides to provide extra protection against the sea.

Norse longships could float in water only a few feet deep. This allowed them to navigate rivers, and they were light enough to be pulled up onto the land. These features made them perfect for raiding. This elegant and powerful design served Viking mariners for 300 years.

The Vikings' oceangoing cargo ships were known as *knarrs*. Large, stable, and strong, these were the first boats in history that could withstand rough, open seas. Broader and heavier than longships, they were partly decked, or covered over, to protect passengers. Their large capacity was designed for cargo. Knarrs were the ships in which Norse explorers and settlers crossed the Atlantic.

The Vikings had a long history of exploring unknown northern coasts and rivers. Sailing close to shore, they used coastal landmarks and identified flora and fauna native to particular areas to calculate their location. By the eighth century, Viking sailors knew the coasts of the Baltic Sea, the North Sea, Britain and northwestern Europe. Viking navigators hugged coastlines where they could, but they sailed willingly in uncharted waters and out of sight of land. Viking ships could stay at sea for days at a time.

Their navigational methods at sea are not fully understood. They did not have compasses or detailed charts. Latitude was their primary guide. They recognized that the Pole Star indicated true north. Thus, they could calculate approximate latitudes by measuring the angle of the star. Norse sailors first sailed along the western Scandinavian coast to the known latitude of their destination, then steered due west until they reached it. They also used dead reckoning. In this method, a voyage is broken down into segments. Each segment is a known direction and number of days' sailing. The *Landnámabók* (Book of settlements), a twelfth-century chronicle of the settlement of Iceland, describes the Vikings' understanding of North Atlantic geography:

> *Wise men report that from Stad in Norway it is a voyage of seven days west to Horn in Iceland, and from Snaefellsnes [in western Iceland] it is four days' sail west to Greenland, at the point where the sea is narrowest. . . . From Reykjanes in southern Iceland it is five days' sail south to Slyne Head in Ireland, and from Langanes in northern Iceland it is four days northward to Svalbard in the Arctic Sea.*

These were crude methods given the uncertainties of winds, currents, tides, and weather, but skillful Viking navigators were thoroughly familiar with conditions along their regular routes and knew how to adjust for them. In shallow waters, sailors could sample the seabed and tell from its composition where they were. At sea, distant cloud formations and the flight patterns of seabirds told them where to find islands. Although the Vikings were expert sailors, sea travel was dangerous. Many ships were lost at sea.

VIKING TACTICS AND STRATEGIES

It was their skill at sea that enabled the Vikings to begin raiding their neighbors in the eighth century. The Viking chieftains needed to maintain their power and status by buying the loyalty of the wealthiest and most powerful inhabitants of their territories. Viking chieftains

THE NORSE SAGAS

Storytelling was popular entertainment among the Norse. Hundreds of their tales have survived in written form, providing a rich record of their history and culture. The word *saga* can be defined in various ways, but as a literary term, it denotes a prose epic, a story of heroes and their deeds.

The Norse sagas often told of heroism, bravery, loyalty, and justice. They also told of romance, revenge, and family feuds. Young lovers, farmers, and outlaws took their place alongside chieftains and royalty in a broad social scene. The Icelanders were the masters of the genre. Storytelling was especially valued in their isolated farmsteads. Generations of Icelanders learned and repeated the sagas from memory until they were finally written down in about 1200. New tales were constantly added, and Norse literature came to include sagas about Norse myths and legends, kings, bishops, family histories, and the Norse expansion into Europe and settlement of Iceland and Greenland.

Although much of the information in the sagas is historically accurate, scholars are not sure of how much fact and invention they contain. Despite this, the Norse sagas present a detailed record of the lives of the Vikings. They are regarded as one of the finest literary achievements of the Middle Ages.

obtained wealth by extortion, piracy, and plunder, and then distributed it to their followers. Where they could extort money without a fight, they did. Otherwise, they attacked in raids that were devastating and quick. During these raids, they took what they wanted and destroyed whatever was left. For three centuries, the Vikings terrorized the people of Ireland, Britain, France, Spain, and the Mediterranean.

Their method was to attack with anything from several to dozens of longships, and dozens to hundreds of men. Viking longships snuck up on their targets, then they quickly closed in on their helpless victims. The raiding Norse slaughtered people in the streets, in their houses, and in church. They captured other people to sell into slavery. They took whatever could be carried away—cash, food, gold and silver, and other luxury items. They even robbed graves and burned entire towns.

The British Isles and western Europe were studded with monasteries, and they were the raiders' earliest targets. The monasteries had accumulated significant wealth in the form of gold and silver, cash, ritual vessels, and other valuables. Most were isolated and undefended. Ports and trading centers were also attacked. They were rich in coins, commodities, and luxury items.

In the mid-ninth century, the Norse adopted two new strategies. Local kings began to pay the Norse to stay away. This protection money is known as tribute. The Vikings needed more than cash and gold, however. Scandinavia's population was outgrowing its territory, and they needed land. The second major strategic change was territorial expansion. Instead of simply raiding, the Vikings began to conquer foreign kingdoms in order to establish their own settlements. By 1060, in fact, they had a kingdom in distant Sicily and southern Italy.

THE NORSE IN THE BRITISH ISLES AND FRANCE

The British Isles were the Vikings' earliest target. The Danes made their first attack on England in about A.D. 790 and continued these attacks for the next two centuries. In addition to its mild climate, England offered rich farmland and opportunities for trade. In A.D. 865, between 500 and 1,000 Vikings, landed on the east coast. Over the next 15 years, they conquered the kingdoms of Northumbria, Mercia, and East Anglia. They killed the English kings and set up their own chieftains across most of northern, central, and eastern England. *The Anglo-Saxon Chronicle* is a history of England written in the ninth century. It gives a melancholy list of attacks:

> *997. In this year the enemy army went round Devonshire to the mouth of the Severn [River], and there plundered and laid waste the land, and killed the inhabitants as also in Cornwall, and also in Wales and Devon . . . the enemy brought about great devastation . . . they burnt and slew everything that was in their path; . . . and took incalculable booty on board their ships. . . .*
> *1003. Exeter was destroyed. . . .*
> *1004. Fleet to Norwich, plundering and burning the whole town. . . .*

The raiders were followed by a wave of Norse, mainly Danish, farmers and traders. They settled a vast area that came to be known as the Danelaw. The Viking immigrants married local people, became Christians, and assimilated. But their language, laws, and customs had a lasting influence on England. The Danish king Canute jointly ruled Scandinavia and England for nearly 20 years (A.D. 1016–1035). His successors were unable to retain the English crown, however, and in the mid-eleventh century, Viking rule in England came to an end.

Ireland, too, was a Viking target. The *Annals of Ulster*, a medieval Irish chronicle, describes how in A.D. 820, "the sea spewed forth floods of foreigners over [Ireland], so that no haven, no landing-place, no stronghold, no fort, no castle might be found, but it was submerged by waves of Vikings and pirates." Ireland became a major Viking trading center. Many of the fortified ports they created there developed into major cities, including Dublin, Waterford, Cork, and Limerick.

The Vikings attacked and settled France as they did England. They looted Paris in A.D. 845. The French monk Ermentarius of Noirmoutier complained in the A.D. 860s, "The endless flood of Vikings never ceases to grow bigger. Everywhere Christ's people are the victims of massacre, burning, and plunder. The Vikings overrun all that lies before them, and none can withstand them."

In A.D. 911, the Norse scored a major coup that was to change the course of both French and English history. In that year, the French king

Charles the Simple paid a Viking leader to protect his lands against other Norse invaders. The Viking chief, Rollo, converted to Christianity and was made a duke. He was given land in northern France. Viking settlers poured in and assimilated, adopting French language and culture. In time, the region was named Normandy (after the Northmen), and its people became the Normans. In 1066, Rollo's descendant William, duke of Normandy (ca. 1028–1087), led a massive invasion of England and defeated King Harold II. Known today as William the Conqueror, he was the first of a Norman line of English kings. William's victory began a second wave of Scandinavian influence on England.

THE VIKINGS MOVE EASTWARD

While the Norwegians and Danes were busy in western Europe, the Swedes were active in the east. Their location on the Baltic Sea made overseas trade easy, and the Norse expansion eastward was based on a wide-reaching exhange of goods. The Swedes soon controlled the trade routes between northern Europe and the Black Sea. Sweden had direct access via the North Sea to the trading centers of western Europe and Britain. Across the Baltic, the Dnieper and Volga river systems wound through eastern Europe. The Swedes followed these rivers into the Black Sea. This gave them access to Constantinople, Baghdad, and the land routes to Asia.

Along these routes, furs, ivory, fish, wool, and slaves were exchanged for gold and silver and luxury items. Millions of medieval Asian and Arabian coins have been found in excavations along the Baltic coast. Among the trading posts the Swedes established were the foundations of Kiev (in present-day Ukraine) and Novgorod (in present-day Russia). Even the name *Russia* comes from the Finnish term for the Swedes, *Ros* or *Rus*. Scandinavian settlers—traders and farmers—followed the traders. By the late tenth century, the Rus were established in Constantinople, the capital of the Byzantine Empire. Known as warriors, the Scandinavians also were sought as mercenaries. They were hired to fight for the Byzantine emperor. In time, they formed his personal bodyguard, the famous Varangian guard.

WESTWARD EXPLORATION AND COLONIZATION

The Vikings' greatest achievements in pure exploration were westward. This part of their story is one of fearless expeditions and peaceful colonization. It took them all the way across the North Atlantic to Iceland and Greenland, and eventually to North America, 500 years before Christopher Columbus (1492).

The Vikings were an adventuresome people. Part of their motivation in sailing the unknown Atlantic Ocean was the challenge. They believed that unknown lands lay to the west. Other important factors were their search for land, their quest for trading opportunities, and a need for raw materials.

From Scandinavia, the summer winds and currents of the North Atlantic favor westward voyages, carrying sailors to Ireland and on to Greenland. From there, the Labrador Current washes southward past modern-day Labrador to Newfoundland, in Canada. This was the path the Vikings followed. The first Viking expedition to reach Iceland was led by Flóki Vilgerdason in about A.D. 860. As the *Book of Settlements* tells it, "Flóki climbed a high mountain and looked north toward the coast, and saw a fjord full of drift-ice. So they called the country Ice-Land, and that has been its name ever since."

Ingolf Arnarson and Leif Hrodmarsson led the first permanent group of Norse settlers to Iceland. They arrived in A.D. 874 with their families, servants, and some Irish slaves. They lived in isolated homesteads, fishing, hunting, and farming sheep and cattle. They were soon joined by others, mostly Norwegians escaping the harsh and overbearing rule of King Harold I Fairhair (ca. A.D. 870–ca. 940). All the good land on Iceland was fully occupied within 60 years. By the end of the tenth century, the population of Iceland was 60,000.

Ships regularly traveled between Iceland and Norway. The Icelanders exported fish and coarse woolen cloth. Because of the climate and poor natural resources, they were dependent on the Norwegian timber, iron, and grain they imported in exchange. The survival of the colony was possible only as long as this trade continued. Famine and hardship were a way of life.

Looking farther west, Erik the Red settled Greenland. He was a violent man, even by Viking standards. In about A.D. 982, having already been twice exiled for manslaughter, he was exiled from Iceland for three years for another killing. During his exile Erik explored Greenland, marking out potential homesteads and farms. Erik named it Greenland because he thought the name would attract settlers. In A.D. 986, he set

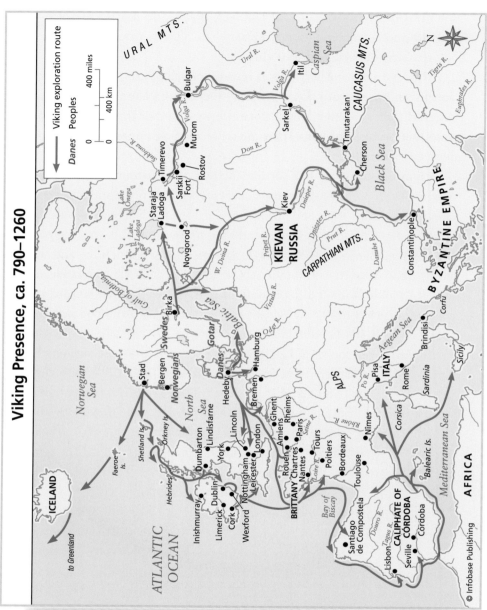

Viking Presence, ca. 790–1260

The Vikings, or Norse, raided and settled large areas of Europe from the late eighth to the thirteenth century. They traveled as far east as Constantinople and Russia's Volga River to as far west as Iceland, Greenland, and Newfoundland.

off to settle Greenland with 25 ships full of Norwegian and Icelandic families and their livestock. Only 14 vessels reached their destination.

Two settlements were built on the more pleasant southwest coast, at present-day Nuuk and Julianehåb. Like the Icelanders, the Greenlanders farmed, hunted, and fished. They depended on imported timber, metals, and grain. Greenland was immediately added to the North Atlantic shipping routes; however, its complete economic dependence doomed its long-term survival as a Norse colony. Norse colonists never numbered more than about 3,000. By the end of the fifteenth century, the last of them left Greenland to the native peoples.

REACHING A NEW WORLD

With their mastery of the North Atlantic nearly complete and their desire to explore still strong, it was perhaps inevitable that the Vikings would eventually reach North America. Historians now agree that Erik's son Leif Eriksson explored the North American coast in about 1000. He sailed westward and first sighted a frozen land he called Helluland (Flatstone-land). This is thought to be Baffin Island, in Canada. It lies southwest of Greenland and north of Hudson Bay. Leif sailed southward along the coast. He came to a wooded region with grasslands and an enormous stretch of sandy beach. He named this place Markland (Forest-land). This was probably Labrador. Sailing farther south, he came to a forested land where wild wheat and grapevines grew. This place he named Vinland (Wine-land). Modern scholars identify the likeliest locale as Newfoundland and suggest that the so-called grapes, which do not grow at this latitude, were in fact some kind of cranberry or red currant. The Norse built themselves shelters and explored during the winter and spring. They returned to Greenland in the summer to tell of the plentiful "grapes," salmon, timber, and grassland they had discovered.

None of the later Norse voyages to North America resulted in permanent settlement. Leif's brother Thorvald led one group of colonists to Vinland in 1003, but after only two winters, hostilities with Native Americans caused them to leave. Another attempt to colonize Vinland came a year or so later. Thorfinn Karlsefni, another Eriksson relative, organized a fleet of three ships. They carried more than 100 settlers and their livestock. They probably spent their first winter on the shore of the mouth of the St. Lawrence River. There, Snorri was born to Thorfinn and his wife, Gudrid, becoming the first European child born in North America.

Thorfinn's group abandoned their settlement after a few years. Like earlier groups, they did not get along with the native peoples. Another expedition to Vinland was led by Erik the Red's daughter Freydis. It failed after she murdered her partner. The Vikings finally gave up on North America sometime between 1010 and 1025. The Viking adventure in North America was judged to be a failure.

THE VIKINGS IN HISTORY

In the 1960s, the Norwegian husband-and-wife team, explorer Helge Ingstad and archaeologist Anne Stine, discovered and excavated the

L'Anse aux Meadows in Newfoundland is a site of Norse settlement in North America. It was excavated in 1960 and is now designated a national historic site. Historians and archaeologists are not sure if this is the Vikings' Vinland.

remains of a Norse settlement at L'Anse aux Meadows, at the northernmost tip of Newfoundland in Canada. The structures there included more than a dozen dwellings, a forge, and an iron smeltery. Material from the site has been scientifically dated to about the year 1000, making this the earliest known European settlement in North America. Whether it was Leif Eriksson's original camp and whether it was a colonial settlement or simply a trading base are open questions.

The Vikings' achievements in the North Atlantic resulted in no significant historical influence. One reason is that Scandinavia and the North Atlantic were so remote and inhospitable that few outsiders went there. Another is that the Viking expansion was not a systematic imperial, military, or commercial effort. Scandinavian settlers were individuals, families, or small groups. The Vikings' North Atlantic colonies were small. Finally, details of their North American explorations were written down, but were not translated for hundreds of years. The details about their shipbuilding, navigation, and seamanship were discovered by others too late for them to be useful.

By contrast, information about Viking raids was widely spread by medieval European historians. These writers were on the receiving end of the terrifying Norse invasions. They described the Vikings simply as thugs who enjoyed violence, murder, and mayhem. Thus, the historical record contained the biases of their European victims. It was not until recently that the Vikings' contributions to sailing technology, exploration, settlement, and trade have been fully appreciated.

5

Muslim Travelers
of the Middle Ages

WITHIN 100 YEARS OF ITS BIRTH IN THE SEVENTH CENTURY, ISLAM
had spread west across North Africa to Morocco and southern Spain.
It reached eastward as far as India. The establishment of Islam in East
Africa and India guaranteed Muslim traders increasingly stable commercial routes. In time, Arab importers and exporters introduced Islam
to coastal China.

Travel literature became popular as Islam extended beyond Arabia.
Between the eighth and eleventh centuries, while medieval Europeans
were still struggling with wars, disease, and intellectual stagnation,
Islamic culture was enjoying its golden age. The study of mathematics, medicine, astronomy, botany, and other sciences flourished. Islamic
arts and architecture were more sophisticated than any found in
Europe. Libraries in Baghdad, Iraq, and Córdoba, Spain, were the intellectual centers of the Arabic world. They were filled with new literature.
Ancient Greek texts were translated, debated, and preserved for future
generations of explorers.

TRAVEL TALES

The first Arab geographers studied and preserved new translations
of ancient Greek authors. These included the philosopher Aristotle
and the Greek-Egyptian astronomer and geographer Ptolemy. Arab
scholarship combined the knowledge of the classical Greeks with
new information from across the Islamic world. Around A.D. 820,
a global geography with maps was compiled by the Baghdad-based

mathematician al-Khwarizmi. (His other works include the mathematical work whose Arabic title provided the modern world with the word *algebra* [*al-jabr*].)

Another geographer was Ibn Khurdadhbih, the postmaster general of Baghdad. In about A.D. 846, he completed the *Book of Roads and Provinces.* This book included maps and descriptions of trade routes by which mail was exchanged across the Muslim world. New writers continually updated travel literature. Similar geographical and travel writing remained a fixture of Arabic scholarship for centuries.

Personal travel accounts soon began to appear in Islamic literature. The first Arab accounts of life in the Far East appeared in observations by Suleiman al-Tajir. Suleiman was a merchant who traded in South Asia and China around A.D. 840. He described Asian seaports, the manufacture of Chinese porcelain, and Islamic trading communities. Later, Al-Ya'qubi's *Book of the Countries* (A.D. 891) was one of the first accounts of both Islamic and foreign lands. Al-Ya'qubi lived in Armenia and parts of modern Iran, Afghanistan, Turkmenistan, and Uzbekistan. After journeying to India, he became the first Arab geographer to write about traveling in Egypt and northwestern Africa. He described countries, governments, and natural resources. He was one of the first sources of information about gold trade routes from sub-Saharan Africa.

POPULAR BOOKS

One of the most popular and influential Islamic geographical works was al-Mas'udi's *Meadows of Gold.* This tenth-century book was based on the work of Ptolemy, but al-Mas'udi's extensive travels enabled him to challenge early Greek misperceptions and advance original ideas.

Al-Mas'udi traveled widely in Persia (present-day Iran) and India. He sailed to Ceylon (Sri Lanka) and possibly China, before eventually returning to Basra, Iraq, by way of Madagascar, Zanzibar, and Oman. Al-Mas'udi completed *Meadows of Gold* in Basra in A.D. 947. He could be blunt, as when he described Egypt as "the old home of the Pharaohs and the dwelling place of tyrants . . . a land where one can become rich but where one does not want to dwell because of troubles and disorders which depress one." Despite this negative portrait, Al-Mas'udi spent his last days in Cairo, perhaps influenced by his observation that "people live there to an advanced age." He wrote constantly until his

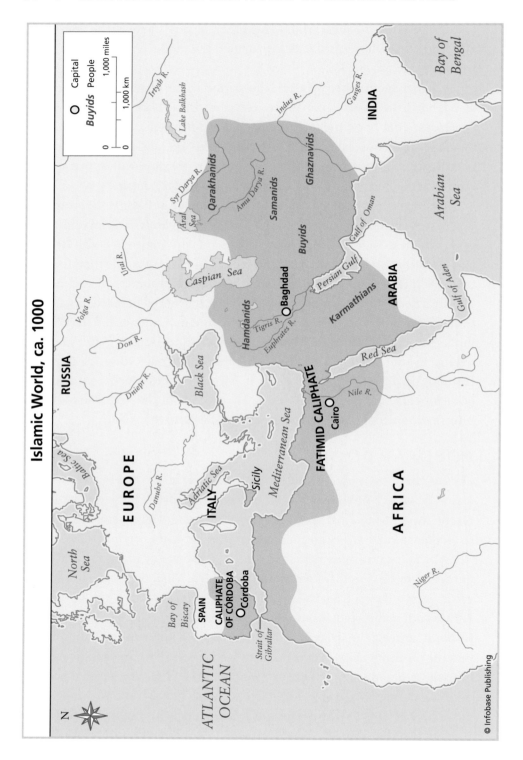

Islamic World, ca. 1000

death in A.D. 957, producing important books about history, geography, travel, and nature. In addition to describing people and lands, he wrote about weather, climate, geology, and the evolution of plants and animals.

The oldest surviving Islamic maps are found in *Description of the Earth* by Ibn Hawqal. Ibn Hawqal left Baghdad in A.D. 943 and spent the next 30 years traveling. He first went to northwest Africa, then visited Spain before traveling south to the desert oasis city of Sijilmassa in modern-day Morocco. This city was an important stop on the gold trade caravan route between the Niger River and the Moroccan port city of Tangier. There, he collected information about Africa south of the Sahara Desert, noting the names of kingdoms along the growing trade route eastward from Morocco to Sudan.

After returning to the Middle East around A.D. 965, Ibn Hawqal headed into central Asia. He visited Bukhara, an important city in Uzbekistan on the silk trade route to China. By A.D. 973, he had passed through Egypt and North Africa to settle in Sicily. He compiled his maps and wrote commentaries on the societies he had encountered. Drawing on travelers' reports and his own reminiscences, Ibn Hawqal's work described people and places. He wrote about the primitive tribes living near Russia's Volga River. He described the sophisticated beauty of Islamic Spain. Although Ibn Hawqal's work contained mistakes, he corrected other long-held misperceptions. Ibn Hawqal could be wildly misleading about peoples beyond Dar-ul-Islam—the Islamic world—but his overall accuracy made his work popular. It was a practical book read by many other travelers.

While some Muslim geographers were content to reach their conclusions in the academic centers of Baghdad and Córdoba, al-Maqdisi was dedicated to learning about the world by seeing it for himself. The author of the classic *Best Divisions for Knowledge of Regions* (A.D. 985), al-Maqdisi was raised in Jerusalem. He did not visit Spain or India but traveled across much of the rest of the Islamic world. He preferred

(opposite page) Ibn Hawqal spent 30 years traveling and recording information about the places and people he had seen in Asia and Africa. He noted the names of kingdoms along the trade routes, and he noticed that there were large numbers of people living in areas the Greeks said were uninhabitable.

to trust his own perceptions and expand upon the work of previous academic geographers. "There is nothing that befalls travelers of which I did not have my share, barring begging and grievous sin," he wrote. He even admitted that he sometimes strayed from Muslim customs:

> At times I have been scrupulously pious; at times I have openly eaten forbidden food. . . . I have ridden in sedans and on horseback, have walked in the sandstorms and snows. I have been in the courtyards of the kings, standing among the nobles; I have lived among the ignorant in the workshops of weavers. What glory and honor I have been given!

For all of the appeal of al-Maqdisi's work as an adventure tale, his attention to detail gave it deeper significance. Details of sociology, politics, archaeology, economics, and even public works were included in his portraits of the places he had seen.

THE GEOGRAPHER AND THE KING

An unusual partnership between a Muslim geographer and a Christian king produced some of the most influential books of the Middle Ages. Al-Idrisi was a Moroccan geographer. He had traveled through much of North Africa, Asia Minor, and Europe and may have gone as far north as England. Around 1138, he was invited to Palermo, Sicily, by the island's ruler Roger II, who was an avid student of geography. Al-Idrisi and Roger II sent investigators abroad to collect geographical and navigational data. This information was studied and compiled at court in Palermo.

Al-Idrisi's most famous map was a planisphere. This type of map shows a sphere (Earth) on a flat surface. Al-Idrisi's version was made of silver and, for its time, was enormous and accurate. The map showed Europe, northern Africa, and western Asia. Al-Idrisi also wrote a book called *Pleasure Excursion of One Eager to Traverse the World's Regions*. He dedicated the book and its collection of maps to Roger II. The king had died shortly after the work's completion in 1154. The book became better known as the *Book of Roger*.

Despite the accuracy of al-Idrisi's cartography and the insights his descriptions still provide into medieval life in the Mediterranean, the *Book of Roger* was neglected for centuries. The planisphere was destroyed by looters. A translation of the book from Arabic into Latin was not published until 1619, so the first European explorers were unaware of its existence. Early copies of the manuscript, however, still survive. The book cemented the Moroccan traveler's reputation as one of the greatest geographers of medieval times.

IBN JUBAYR

The *rihla* of Ibn Jubayr became a model for other travelers' memoirs in the later medieval period. While serving as secretary to the governor of Granada, Spain, in 1182, he was forced by his employer to drink seven cups of wine. This action violated the laws of Islam. To make up for his act, the governor gave Ibn Jubayr seven cups full of gold coins. He used the gold to fund a pilgrimage to Mecca. His journals of his hajj were of great value to geographers and travelers.

ISLAM, TRAVEL, AND GEOGRAPHY

Even more than trade, religion inspired Muslims to travel and study geography. One of the five duties, or "pillars," of Islamic faith requires that every Muslim pray five times daily while facing Mecca, the holiest of Islamic cities, located in present-day western Saudi Arabia. Determining the precise direction of Mecca from points across an increasingly large Islamic world made geography a basic and legitimate field of study.

One duty of Islam requires every Muslim to visit Mecca once in a lifetime, if possible. The duty of making this pilgrimage, called the hajj, added fresh importance to the study of navigation and other practical sciences of value to pilgrims wishing to visit sacred sites associated with the prophet Muhammad. The religious duty of Muslims to extend hospitality to one another made travel safer. While normal hardships remained, travelers expected a warm reception from fellow Muslims wherever they traveled in the Islamic world. Treatment of Muslims in foreign lands was a constant topic, both in the writings of travelers and in geographies compiled by nontraveling scholars.

Ibn Jubayr left Spain in 1183. He first went to Egypt. There, he saw one of the "seven wonders" of the ancient world, the Lighthouse of Alexandria. In his journal, Ibn Jubayr described the nearly 400-foot (121.9-meter) landmark. Its large tower and mirrored light guided mariners:

> *It can be seen for more than seventy miles, and is of great antiquity. It is most strongly built in all directions and competes with the skies in height. Description of it falls short, the eyes fail to comprehend it, and words are inadequate, so vast is the spectacle.*

After completing his pilgrimage to Mecca, Ibn Jubayr returned to Spain. He traveled by way of the seaport of Acre on the coast of present-day Israel. Ibn Jubayr set sail for Spain in late 1184. When his ship was wrecked, he found himself in Sicily, which was then ruled by Christian Normans. Ibn Jubayr wrote about his experiences after his return to Granada in 1185. He described Palermo as an "elegant city, magnificent and gracious, and seductive to look upon. Proudly set between its open spaces and plains filled with gardens, with broad roads and avenues, it dazzles the eyes with its perfection." He recorded the practices of Christians in countries he visited. "The Christian women of this city," he noted of Palermo, "follow the fashion of Muslim women, are fluent of speech, wrap their cloaks about them, and are veiled."

TRAVELS OF IBN BATTUTAH

Arab civilization faced disaster in the early thirteenth century when Mongol invaders swept southwest across Asia Minor. They destroyed everything in their path. The Mongol conquerors soon adopted Islam as their faith, but not before burning Baghdad in 1258. Libraries full of maps and books written during Islam's golden age were lost in the fire. The greatest *rihla* of the Middle Ages, however, had yet to be written.

The author was Ibn Battutah. His journeys covered an astonishing 75,000 miles (120,701 km) over roughly 30 years. In 1325, when he was 21, Ibn Battutah left his native Morocco to make the hajj to Mecca. After accomplishing this goal, he continued to travel. After visiting Baghdad, he made his way down the Red Sea to Yemen. He then sailed to the east coast of Africa, stopping in present-day Somalia and Kenya.

Although Ibn Battuta's *Rihla* exaggerates at times, it is still considered the most accurate account of some parts of the world in the fourteenth century. After the publication of his book little was known about Battuta, including his appearance. Here a recent amateur illustration is shown with a beard, his only known physical characteristic.

Ibn Battutah returned to Mecca for other pilgrimages, but he always went by a different route. Using Mecca as a base, he visited great cities such as Damascus and Jerusalem. He relied on hospitality shown to pilgrims by other Muslims, from common citizens to emperors curious to hear about the wonders he had seen. Some hosts returned the favor. In eastern Turkey, a sultan showed Ibn Battutah a meteorite:

> He said to me, "Have you ever seen a stone that has fallen from the sky?" I replied, "No, nor ever heard of one." "Well," he said, "a stone fell from the sky outside this town." ... A great black stone was brought, very hard and with a glitter in it, I reckon its weight was about a hundredweight. The sultan sent for stone breakers, and four of them came and struck it all together four times over with iron hammers, but made no impression on it. I was amazed.

In 1333, after traveling throughout central Asia, Ibn Battutah reached India. After serving as a judge in Delhi for eight years, he was sent by the city's sultan as an ambassador to the Mongol emperor of China. The trip took Ibn Battutah to the Maldive Islands, Ceylon, Sumatra, and probably China. His tour of China is the least well documented of his journeys, but it is generally believed that he reached his destination, the Chinese court in Beijing.

He returned to Morocco in 1349, but he was soon on the move again. In 1352, he headed south across the Sahara Desert by camel, passing bleak salt mines and treacherous sandy wastelands. He eventually reached the west African kingdom of Mali, where he met with the sultan. He described the ruler's African subjects as moral, law abiding, and peaceful. He also noted the traveling conditions, religions, food, customs, wildlife, laws, and relationships between men and women. He described enormous baobab trees, whose shade was wide enough to shelter an entire caravan:

> Some of these trees are rotted in the interior and the rain-water collects in them, so that they serve as wells and the people drink of the water inside them. In others there are bees and honey, which is collected by the people. I was surprised to find inside

one tree, by which I passed, a man, a weaver, who had set up his loom in it and was actually weaving.

Ibn Battutah returned north in 1353. The Moroccan sultan commanded him to put the story of his journeys into writing. A professional scribe named Ibn Juzayy was appointed to help. Ibn Battutah dictated his experiences to the young writer, who edited and polished the prose. The result was a travel narrative relating an extraordinary life. Its title was *A Gift to the Observers Concerning the Curiosities of the Cities and the Marvels Encountered in Travels.* It is commonly referred to as Ibn Battutah's *Rihlah.* The book remains one of the great sourcebooks of the Middle Ages.

IBN KHALDUN

Like many Muslim writers, Ibn Khaldun was not just a geographer. He traveled and lived in Algeria, Tunisia, Spain, and Egypt. In the 1370s, he wrote *Muqaddimah.* This was the first volume of his history of the world. He wrote about geography, politics, the environment, business, science, poetry, Islamic society, and the rise and decline of civilizations. Much of what he described came from his travels.

Ibn Khaldun was one of the last great Muslim intellectual travelers of the Middle Ages. These Muslim travelers and geographers significantly increased humankind's knowledge of Earth's geography. Not only had they saved the writings of classical Greek geographical theorists, Muslim travelers and scholars also created their own lasting legacy of geographical literature, increasingly accurate maps, and cultural commentaries on the medieval societies of the Eastern Hemisphere.

6

Europeans Seeking Asia

UNTIL THE MID-THIRTEENTH CENTURY, EUROPEANS BARELY traveled outside the ancient Greek and Roman world and knew little about central Asia, India, or East Asia. Europeans learned of eastern lands from the Bible, legends, and fabulous tales of heroes, especially stories about Alexander the Great (356–323 B.C.), king of Macedonia. From these sources and trade, they knew Asia only as the source of luxury imports such as silk and spices.

THE MONGOL EMPIRE

The Mongol conquest of Asia and eastern Europe provided an opportunity for the Europeans to extend their eastern horizon. The Mongols, whom the Europeans called Tartars, were unorganized nomads of the central Asian steppes (plains) until Genghis Khan assumed supreme power over them in 1206. He reigned until 1227 with the goal of world domination. His tens of thousands of Mongol troops were expert horsemen and archers. Famous for their savagery, the Mongols rapidly overran a patchwork of kingdoms from northern and eastern China westward to Persia and eastern Europe. Mongol armies conquered Russia in 1237–1240. By 1241, they were camped outside of Vienna. By this time, the son of Genghis, Ögödei, had succeeded his father, their supreme leader. Only his death, in December 1241, caused the Mongols to withdraw from Europe. Nevertheless, Genghis Khan's ambition was realized. His grandsons Mangu Khan and Kublai Khan ruled over the largest empire the world has ever known. It stretched from the China Sea to the Mediterranean Sea.

The Silk Roads were the ancient overland caravan routes linking the Middle East with the Far East. Under Mongol rule, they came under political control for the first time in history. The Mongols, like the Chinese before them, closely supervised roadways and facilities for travelers. The transportation of goods along the overland routes—traditionally slow, expensive, and dangerous—became much safer. Long barred by hostile Islamic states from the lucrative Far Eastern trade routes across northern Africa and southwest Asia, the Europeans were quick to seize their opportunity.

European rulers wanted to make direct contact with the new empire to their east. They had several motives. They needed to know how serious a threat the Mongols were. Their armies continued to harass eastern Europe until 1290. The thirteenth-century English historian Matthew Paris vividly described the "terrible destruction," "fire and carnage," and "ravaging and slaughtering" that were taking place to the east. Europeans also sought an alliance in which the Mongols would fight with them against the Muslims, who then controlled Jerusalem and the Holy Land. Europeans also badly wanted direct access to the overland trade routes to the fabulous wealth of China. The Silk Road was their only opportunity to participate in the lucrative Far Eastern trade, for they had no means of rounding Africa by ship in order to gain direct access to the sea routes to the Far East.

Finally, the Europeans hoped to convert the Mongols to Christianity. The Mongols were Shamanists, that is, believers in invisible spirits that controlled the physical world. They were tolerant of all faiths, however, allowing the many Muslims, Jews, Buddhists, and others who lived among them to practice their religions freely. Europeans hoped that the Mongol ruler, if not his subjects, might be converted.

FATHER JOHN PLANO CARPINI'S MISSION

The first western European emissaries to the Mongol court were Christian friars assigned to diplomatic and political duties in addition to their religious role. The Mongols had destroyed about three-quarters of Hungary, and the Hungarian king Béla IV was on the front lines. He sent emissaries to the Mongols to gather intelligence. Béla's last ambassador, the Dominican friar Julian, returned with some information in 1236–1237. His news was not good. The Mongols simply demanded submission and nothing less would do.

The Mongols, who controlled much of Asia in the later Middle Ages, were nomads. They lived in their homes, or yurts, year-round. When it was time to move, the structure could collapse into a small enough bundle to fit on a pack animal and then set up again in half an hour. This photograph is of a Mongolian family outside of their yurt in 1935.

Pope Innocent IV was eager to bring Asia into the Christian fold. In 1245, only four years after the Mongols retreated from the outskirts of Vienna, he sent two separate Franciscan embassies to the great khan. Their orders were to gather intelligence about the Mongols, to protest the bloody invasion of Europe, and to convert the Mongols to Christianity. One embassy failed. The leader of the other, the Italian Franciscan friar John Plano Carpini (ca. 1180–1252), became the first European to travel the land routes to central Asia. His journey from France to Mongolia and back lasted two-and-a-half-years. He covered 15,000 miles (24,140 km).

Carpini and his companions left Lyon, France, on Easter Day in 1245. It took them nearly a year to reach Batu Khan's camp near the Volga River. Under Batu Khan's rule, the western Mongols had brutally massacred the Russians and Hungarians. Batu Khan, nevertheless, gave Carpini supplies, guides, and fast Mongol horses. These helped Carpini reach the court of the great khan. Carpini covered the last 3,000 miles (4,828 km) of his journey in just 106 days. He crossed deserts, barren plains, and high mountains and endured bitter cold, unappetizing foods, and humiliating treatment from his hosts. The friar reached the imperial camp near the Mongol capital of Karakorum in central Mongolia on July 22, 1246. He was just in time to witness the election and enthronement of Güyük as the new great khan. Carpini spent four months at the Mongol imperial court.

He delivered a letter from Pope Innocent IV to the great khan. "We are . . . greatly surprised," the pope wrote, "that you, as We have learned, have attacked and cruelly destroyed many countries belonging to Christians and many other peoples." The letter invited the khan to be baptized and accept supreme papal authority.

Güyük's reply, dated November 1246, was blunt. He did not understand either the pope's distress or his claim to sovereignty. "Through the power of God, all empires from sunrise to sunset have been given to us, and we own them," wrote the great khan. "You personally, at the head of the Kings, you shall come, one and all, to pay homage to me, and to serve me." If the pope disobeyed this divine order, Güyük wrote, "we shall know that you are our enemies." Leaving Mongolia that same month, Carpini carried the khan's letter on the strenuous year-long journey home. "We . . . traveled right through the winter," he later wrote. "We often had to lie in snow in the wilderness."

Shortly after his return, Carpini submitted to the pope a formal report of his mission. He described the skeletons and burned-out towns the Mongols had left behind in eastern Europe. He had found the Mongols to be violent, arrogant, dishonest, sly, greedy, drunken, and filthy in their personal habits. He tried to put aside his contempt, however, and write objectively.

Carpini's *Historia Mongalorum* (History of the Mongols), was written in Latin in the form of a letter to the pope. It was a record of the Mongols' religion, politics, military, laws, customs, and history. It was the first European work ever written about central Asia or China. It also was the first European travel writing that relied on personal observation and fact. The *Historia* is a valuable portrait of the Mongols soon after the foundation of their empire. It set the standard by which similar books would be judged.

WILLIAM OF RUBRUCK'S JOURNEY

William of Rubruck (ca. 1215–ca. 1295) followed in Carpini's footsteps. A French Franciscan friar, he volunteered for an embassy to the Mongols representing Louis IX of France after accompanying the French king on the failed Seventh Crusade (1248–1250). His mission was similar to Carpini's. He was to gather information about the Mongol's military, seek an alliance, and convert the Mongols to Christianity.

William left Constantinople on May 7, 1253. He carried Turkish and Arabic translations of a letter from the French king to the Mongol prince Sartach. William sailed to the Black Sea, a two-week voyage. He then continued overland with oxen and carts, reaching Sartach's camp at the end of July. Sartach referred him to his father, Batu Khan, who in turn sent William's party on to Mangu, the great khan. They endured a difficult journey on horseback over the same route Carpini had followed. They slept "always under the open skies or under our wagons." "There was no end to hunger and thirst, cold and exhaustion," William later wrote. "We had run out of wine, and the water was so churned up by the horses it was undrinkable. If we hadn't had biscuit and God's help, we would possibly have died."

William reached Mangu's camp on December 27. He stayed for six months at the imperial court at Karakorum. "When I found myself among [the Mongols]," he recalled, "it seemed to me as if I were in another world." The khan treated him politely, but as Carpini had before him, William found the Mongols coarse, rude, arrogant, untrustworthy, and greedy. They asked "shamelessly . . . like dogs" for gifts and shares of whatever he had. Some questioned him about the spoils they might be able to seize in France.

Despite his disgust at his hosts, William was patient. He spent the summer of 1254 at Karakorum. He compared the city unfavorably with Paris. The Mongol capital had 12 temples to Mongol gods, two mosques, and one Christian church. It had markets and palaces, and separate residential quarters for Muslims and Chinese. During his time there, William participated in public debates between Christians, Muslims, and Buddhists, but primarily spoke with Europeans who lived among the Mongols. Most of them were slaves or artisans captured during western raids.

Finally permitted by the khan to depart, William left Karakorum on August 15, 1254. He carried a letter from the khan demanding the submission of the king of France. The friar's journey took him back to Batu's camp on the Volga River, along the western side of the Caspian Sea, across the Caucasus Mountains, and westward through Asia Minor. He reached the Mediterranean coast in May 1255. He had traveled more than 9,000 miles (14,484 km) during his two-year absence.

WILLIAM OF RUBRUCK'S REPORT

On his return, William immediately wrote a lively and detailed account of his experience. It took the form of a letter to Louis IX. His report is usually referred to as *The Journey of William of Rubruck to the Eastern Parts of the World.* It contains a vivid record of the hardships of medieval travel. It also contains valuable geographical, historical, and ethnographical information about medieval central Asia. Perhaps the finest work of travel writing to survive from the Middle Ages, it was little known until the sixteenth century.

William made important geographical discoveries. He was the first European to correct the mistaken belief that the Caspian Sea was an inlet of the ocean. He also described the size and course of the Volga River.

In addition, he described Mongol culture. William analyzed the complex life at court. He noted the khan's devious practice of playing rival priests off each other, "for he believed in none . . . and they all follow his court as flies do honey, and he gives to all, and they all believe that they are his favorites, and they all prophesy blessings to him." This did not seem promising for the Christian conversion effort.

William found little to admire among the Mongols. Yet, he was deeply interested in their languages and arts, their clothing and food ("they eat mice and all kinds of rats which have short tails"), and their yurts. These were large circular felt tents that were carried fully erect from place to place on 20-foot-wide (6-meter-wide) ox-drawn carts. William reported on their judicial system and seasonal migrations. He observed their hunting techniques, division of men's and women's work, and marriage customs ("no one among them has a wife unless he buys her"). He included details about Mongol treatment of the sick and the dead. He described feasts, manners ("quite disgusting"), and superstitions. William did not think them unconquerable: "I would, if permitted, preach war against them, to the best of my ability, throughout the world," the friar advised the French king.

William's contact with Chinese residents of Karakorum gave him valuable information about East Asia. He mentioned paper money 50 years before Marco Polo and was the first European to refer to Chinese writing. William was also the first to fully describe the beliefs and rites of Buddhism, Lamaism (a Tibetan form of Buddhism led by the Dalai Lama), Shamanism, and Nestorian Christianity (a form of Christianity that had spread eastward from the Middle East).

OTHER TRAVELERS BETWEEN EUROPE AND ASIA

Two later missionaries also made important contributions to medieval Europeans' knowledge of Asia. John of Montecorvino (1247–1328), an Italian Franciscan friar and longtime missionary to the Middle East, traveled to the great khan on behalf of Pope Nicholas IV in 1291. Along the way he founded the first Roman Catholic missions in southern India, and he sent back the first detailed account of that region by a European. In 1294, he arrived in the Mongol capital of Khanbalik (or Cambaluc, also known as the present-day city of Beijing.) John of Montecorvino would spend the rest of his life there. He eventually became the first Roman Catholic archbishop of China.

Friar Odoric of Pordenone (ca. 1286–1331), another Italian Franciscan, was sent as a missionary to Asia in about 1317–1318. He traveled overland through Asia Minor and Persia. He then boarded a ship at the Persian Gulf port of Hormuz. He visited India, Sumatra, Java, Borneo, and Southeast Asia, finally reaching China in about 1323. Odoric traveled extensively there. He spent the years 1325–1328 at the Cambaluc mission founded by John of Montecorvino. Although he failed to convert the great khan, Yuan emperor Tai Ding Di, Odoric baptized 20,000 others. On his overland journey home, Odoric became the first European to travel through Tibet, visiting Buddhist monasteries there. His *Itinerarium* (Itinerary) was a memoir of his extensive travels and the

William of Rubruck kneels before the Mongolian chief, Mangu Khan, in 1251. The report of his travels, which was divided into 40 chapters, gives great detail about the Mongol peoples and scientific descriptions of central Asia. His report has been compared in importance to Marco Polo's.

first European record of a number of Asian habits and customs including the Chinese practice of binding girls' feet. Odonic's book was one of the most widely read travel books of the Middle Ages.

If thirteenth-century Asians traveled to Europe, they left little record of their activity. One exception was Rabban Bar Sauma (ca. 1220–1294). He was a Nestorian Christian teacher and the first known Chinese-born traveler to Europe. He was living in Baghdad in 1287 when Arghun, the regional khan of Persia, appointed him ambassador to the Christian European monarchs. Arghun was seeking a military alliance against the Muslims. Bar Sauma traveled in Italy and France and met with Philip IV of France, Edward I of England, and Pope Nicholas IV. He then returned home. Bar Sauma's diary of his journey was written in Persian. It provided a rare outsider's view of medieval Europe.

THE CRUSADES

Between 1096 and 1270, many thousands of European Christians waged war against Muslims in the Holy Land and the Near East. Their expeditions are known as the Crusades. The European invasions were a response to several broad historical developments. The early eleventh century was a period of increased prosperity, population growth, and relative political stability in Europe. Pilgrims took to the roads in record numbers, and mass pilgrimages to Jerusalem became common. In 1071, however, Jerusalem fell to hostile Muslims, the Seljuk Turks. The Byzantine Greek emperor, Alexius I, appealed to Pope Urban II as a fellow Christian for help in ousting the Seljuks, who had closed the overland routes to Jerusalem. Anxious to recapture Jerusalem, restore European access to the Holy Land, and protect Christian holy sites and the pilgrims who visited them, the pope came to the eastern emperor's aid.

Tens of thousands of European knights and infantrymen traveled to the Holy Land to oust the Muslims. About 100,000 Europeans fought in the First Crusade. Informal groups went, too, as the fighting attracted criminals who were undisciplined and poorly equipped.

The Crusades lasted for two centuries. The fortunes of the Christian and Muslim armies and the holy places themselves rose and

IMPACT OF THESE CONTACTS

The Christian missionaries who traveled to Mongol China in the thirteenth and early fourteenth centuries accomplished one of the greatest feats of medieval European exploration. They opened direct overland routes from Europe to Asia for the first time. They brought the civilizations of the East and West face to face. Their written accounts of their journeys replaced age-old legends about Asia with factual information. Within only 70 years of the first failed papal embassy to Asia in 1177, a huge region previously unknown to Europeans—central Asia, South Asia, and East Asia—became known in the West. Europeans filled in blanks on their maps.

These travelers combined the functions of missionaries, diplomats, spies, and explorers. The geographical knowledge they brought back to

fell. Control of Jerusalem changed hands repeatedly. Cities were destroyed, and many people were killed. In the end, the Egyptian sultan al-Ashraf expelled the Christians in 1291.

The Crusades added to the geographical knowledge of Europeans. The Europeans' foothold in the Middle East enabled them to contact the Mongols. The several states Crusaders established in the Holy Land and Constantinople provided a base of operations for Europeans. The Venetians' easternmost trading posts, for example, were starting points for Christian missionaries to China. Later, they were points of departure for explorers such as Marco Polo and his uncles.

One final result of the Crusades was that the Islamic states closed ranks against Christendom. Centuries of Islamic religious tolerance ended. European travelers and merchants were banned from Muslim-controlled ports and were not allowed on overland routes in North Africa and southwest Asia. Forced to seek other routes, Europeans developed a northerly overland route and explored direct sea routes from Europe. The success of both of these efforts had enormous consequences for European—and world—history.

Europe was important. Just as significant were the political and cultural ties they established. Their accounts guided European traders right to the source of Chinese silks and spices. By the fourteenth century, European scholars were drawing on Western, Persian, and Mongol sources alike. Mongol embassies to the west were becoming routine.

In 1368, the Mongols were defeated and replaced by the isolationist Ming dynasty in China. Hostile Islamic states sprang up in central Asia and closed overland routes. These developments stimulated English, Spanish, Portuguese, and Dutch mariners to discover a sea route to the riches of the Far East. This goal was to elude them for more than 100 years.

7

Marco Polo and His Travels

MARCO POLO LIVED FROM ABOUT 1254–1324. HE WAS THE MOST famous explorer of the Middle Ages and arguably one of the greatest explorers of all time. His name has become synonymous with traveling long distances through exotic regions. The broad outline of his trip to Mongol China is well known. At the age of 17, he journeyed with his father and uncle, the Venetian merchants Niccolò and Maffeo Polo, to the court of the great Mongol emperor Kublai Khan. After a three-year journey overland through central Asia, they arrived at the imperial court in northern China. Young Marco entered the khan's service. During the 17 years he spent in China, he traveled throughout the empire. He finally returned to Venice with the elder Polos in 1295, having been away for 24 years.

THE POLOS AND MARCO'S TRAVELS

When Marco Polo reached home at age 41, he was probably the best-traveled person in the world. He had spent years on the roads, tracks, and seas of Asia. He had been a privileged insider in a vast, rich eastern realm that few Europeans had ever heard of and fewer still had visited. His knowledge of the Mongolian and Persian languages allowed him to penetrate Asian cultures in a way no European before him had done. His adventures were described in *The Description of the World* (popularly known as the *Travels*). This book provided Europeans with of new knowledge about China, South Asia, Southeast Asia, Indonesia, Japan, and the lands of the Indian Ocean.

In all the attention deservedly given to Marco Polo, it is often overlooked that his father and uncle, Niccolò and Maffeo, had traveled to China before. In 1260, the two brothers were in Constantinople when war stopped them from returning to Venice. They decided to travel eastward instead. After a four-year overland journey, they reached the court of Kublai Khan. They spent four years there. When the Polos did return home, they came as the great khan's ambassadors to the pope. They did not write about their experiences or tell their story to someone who would. Without this record, they were denied an important place in the history of exploration. Although they must have seen some of the same things that Marco did 20 years later, no evidence of their experience survived. Similarly, little is known about what the elder Polos did during their long second stay in China with Marco. Marco Polo's book, on the other hand, gained him his starring role in history.

THE ITINERARY

The Description of the World, or the *Travels,* divides Marco Polo's stay into several itineraries. These itineraries focus on regions unknown to his European readers. The book describes in detail the Polos' eastward journey along the ancient trading routes of the Silk Roads through central Asia, traveled for centuries by the Arabs, Persians, Jews, and Chinese. They were still largely unknown to Europeans.

The Polos left Palestine in 1271. They traveled through Asia Minor and crossed the Persian deserts in modern-day Iraq and Iran. They spent a year in Afghanistan recovering from illness, perhaps malaria. The *Travels* describes the high, mountainous Pamir plateau, northern India, Tibet, and the punishing month-long crossing of the Gobi Desert. Three-and-a-half years after leaving Venice, the travelers reached the Mongols' summer capital of Shangdu (Shang-tu) in northern China in 1274. Little is known of Marco's specific activities in China. He clearly traveled to the southern regions and the east coast of the country, since these areas are described in the *Travels.*

(opposite page) Marco Polo, along with his father Niccoló and his uncle Maffeo, traveled to the Mongol empire in hopes of converting the Mongols to Christianity. Marco's account of his 24-year journey describes their travels along the Silk Roads and to other regions previously unknown to Europeans.

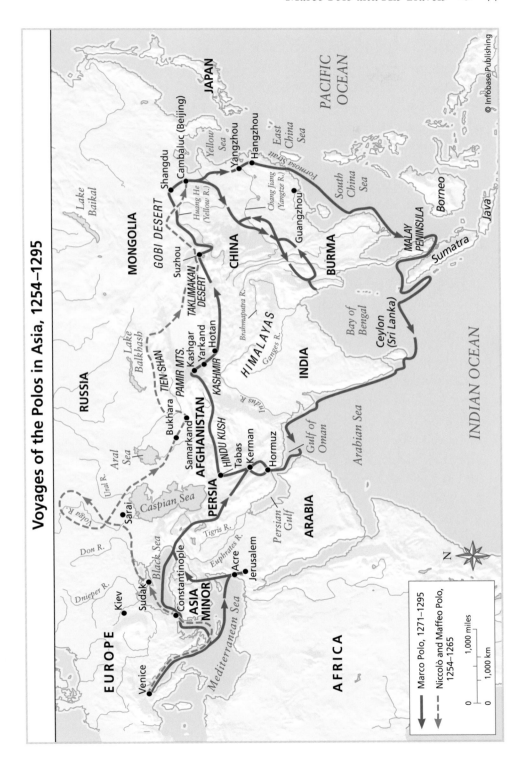

Voyages of the Polos in Asia, 1254–1295

EUROPE

Venice

Kiev

Dnieper R.

Sudak

Black Sea

Constantinople

ASIA MINOR

Acre

Jerusalem

Don R.

Euphrates R.

Tigris R.

Mediterranean Sea

AFRICA

ARABIA

Persian Gulf

Sarai

Volga R.

Ural R.

Aral Sea

Caspian Sea

PERSIA

Tabas

Kerman

Hormuz

Gulf of Oman

Arabian Sea

INDIAN OCEAN

Bukhara

Samarkand

AFGHANISTAN

HINDU KUSH

KASHMIR

Kashgar

Yarkand

Hotan

PAMIR MTS.

TIEN SHAN

Lake Balkhash

RUSSIA

Lake Baikal

MONGOLIA

GOBI DESERT

TAKLIMAKAN DESERT

Suzhou

Shangdu

Cambaluc (Beijing)

JAPAN

Yellow Sea

Yangzhou

Hangzhou

East China Sea

Huang He (Yellow R.)

Chang Jiang (Yangtze R.)

Guangzhou

CHINA

Formosa Strait

HIMALAYAS

Brahmaputra R.

Ganges R.

Indus R.

INDIA

Bay of Bengal

Ceylon (Sri Lanka)

BURMA

South China Sea

MALAY PENINSULA

Sumatra

Borneo

Java

PACIFIC OCEAN

N

Marco Polo, 1271–1295

Niccolò and Maffeo Polo, 1254–1265

1,000 miles

1,000 km

0

0

© Infobase Publishing

The Polos asked for permission to return home in about 1290. Kublai Khan was growing old, and the Italians knew their position would be insecure after he died. They were allowed to accompany a Mongol princess who was being sent to become the wife of Arghun, the regional khan of Persia. Fourteen ships full of courtiers and crew members—also carrying, of course, the Polos and the princess—sailed from China. It took them three years to reach Persia. The *Travels* describes places on the way: Sumatra, Java, the Malay Peninsula, Ceylon, India, and the great Persian port of Hormuz. It also describes the Indian Ocean trade routes, then controlled by Arab and Hindu merchants.

THE MONGOLS

During the Polos' stay, China was in an extraordinary phase in its long history. For the first time, much of China was under foreign rule. Those rulers were Mongols. Originally a loose confederation of more or less nomadic northern Asian tribes, the Mongols had been unified by Genghis Khan during his reign from 1206 to 1227. Dreaming of world conquest, Genghis Khan led his huge armies southward, then westward, at lightning speed, conquering all before him. He eventually ruled a vast empire from northern China to the Caspian Sea. After Genghis's death, his lands were divided among his descendants. Each one ruled four smaller and more manageable empires called khanates and their ruler's were called khans. The largest khanate was China and its khan was the great khan, or supreme ruler.

When Niccolò and Maffeo Polo arrived in China on their first visit in about 1260, Genghis Khan's grandson, Kublai Khan, was great khan. He controlled a vast empire stretching from Korea across China, Mongolia, Tibet, and central Asia to Persia, and Russia. Most Europeans were terrified of the Mongols, and with good cause. In 1238, the Mongols had overrun Moscow. Next they overpowered European armies in present-day Poland and Hungary, then they moved against Vienna. Only their sudden withdrawal to Mongolia to elect a new great khan in 1241 ended the immediate threat to western Europe. The Europeans thought the Mongols were savages. Medieval Christian teachings and maps reinforced this view by placing Jerusalem at the center of the world. Those who lived at the edge of the world, like the Mongols, were officially classified as barbarians.

MARCO POLO AND THE GREAT KHAN

Marco Polo, however, was seduced by the power and splendor of the Mongol emperor and his court when he arrived there in 1274. He admired Kublai Khan. As Polo explained in his *Travels*, "[I]n respect to number of subjects, extent of territory, and amount of revenue, he surpasses every sovereign that has heretofore been or that now is in the world." In general, Polo painted Kublai Khan as a benign ruler, paying little attention to the great khan's famous bloodthirstiness.

The historical Kublai Khan was curious about the world and sought exchanges with European rulers and religious leaders. The Mongols' unification of central Asia allowed Europeans to travel the overland routes to East Asia safely. European traders, missionaries, and ambassadors developed a regular flow of communication with China in the thirteenth century. When they first reached China in the 1260s, Niccolò and Maffeo Polo were not the first Europeans to appear at the Mongol court. Friars John Plano Carpini and William of Rubruck are but two of the best known of other early visitors.

Having obtained his throne by conquest, Kublai Khan trusted outsiders more than the Chinese and, therefore, employed large numbers of foreigners. On their second trip to China with Marco, the elder Polos served as ambassadors between Kublai Khan and Pope Gregory X. Marco Polo also seems to have worked for the great khan in some minor administrative capacity.

MARCO POLO'S MONGOL EMPIRE

Marco Polo enjoyed the wealth and sophistication of China. The *Travels* tells of the lavish banquets, decorations, costumes, and amusements of Kublai Khan's court. It cites the emperor's 12,000 barons and 12,000 mounted bodyguards, his four wives' 40,000 attendants, and his 300,000-strong army. Because these numbers were probably exaggerated, people created an ironic nickname for his book: *Il Milione* (meant "the million marvels"). Marco Polo marveled at Shangdu, with its marble palace and gilded halls. He described the Mongol's winter capital at Cambaluc (Beijing) and its royal warehouses were filled with gold, silver, and jewels. Polo called Hangzhou, "the finest and most splendid city in the world." It was home to more than one million people and was famous for its richly ornamented buildings, beautiful lake, gardens, canals, bridges, markets, and fine artisans. Hangzhou was indeed one of the wonders of the medieval world. It was unknown to Europeans until Marco Polo described it to them.

Polo was also fascinated by everyday life in China. He was raised in one of the greatest trading centers of Europe and had a keen eye for the material world. The *Travels* reports on China's geography, currency, industry, and crops. It lists resources such as gems, metals, and minerals. It details native plants and methods of transportation. Polo was interested in recording Asia's many differences from Europe.

Thirteenth-century Europe was politically divided. Its small states were in constant conflict. Its people were uneducated, poor, and hungry. By contrast, China was a land of plenty. It was rich in silver and ruby mines, jade, coal, and oil. The economy had a strong base of agriculture, manufacturing, fine craftsmanship, and trade. China's towns were bustling and its grand cities were "planned out with a degree of precision and beauty impossible to describe."

Thousands of clean, comfortable post houses lined China's well-paved and well-marked roads. They housed travelers and the 200,000 horses that carried official messages throughout the empire. China's roads and waterways, including the 1,000-mile-long (1,609.3-km-long) Grand Canal, were filled with traffic. Of the great Chang Jiang (Yangtze River) the *Travels* reported, "the total volume of traffic exceeds all the rivers of the Christians put together and their seas into the bargain."

Mongol China was a vast and diverse empire. Polo kept careful notes about its ethnic groups, languages, religions, diet, and marriage customs. The mundane details of Chinese life seemed strange to Europeans. The *Travels* reported a custom among the people of one province:

When one man has had a son, and another man a daughter, although both may have been dead for some years, they have a practice of contracting a marriage between their deceased children and of bestowing the girl upon the youth. They at the same time paint upon pieces of paper human figures to represent attendants with horses and other animals, clothing of all kinds, money, and every article of furniture; and all these, together with the marriage contract, which is regularly drawn up, they commit to flames, in order that through the medium of the smoke (as

*they believe) these things may be conveyed to their children in
the other world and that they may become husband and wife in
due form.*

Polo's European readers learned how crocodiles were caught, buffalo meat picked, and tattoos applied. Some Asians, they read, had gold-plated teeth. The Chinese people themselves, according to Polo, were cheerful, polite, intelligent, clean, hardworking, honest, and prosperous. They were sophisticated in ways that must have puzzled Europeans. Instead of metal coins, the Chinese used paper money. Each square piece was hand-signed and stamped by imperial officials. The Chinese burned coal for fuel. They told time with water clocks. Wonders abounded in the *Travels*. Yet the author insisted, "Not the twentieth part have I described."

THE CREATION AND IMPACT OF MARCO POLO'S BOOK

Marco Polo returned to Venice in 1295. He felt a responsibility to publicize such amazing discoveries after he returned home. Sometime later, Polo was captured in a sea battle between the city-states of Venice and Genoa. He was imprisoned in Genoa. Among his fellow prisoners was Rustichello from Pisa, Italy, a writer of popular romances. Polo dictated his story to Rustichello, who then translated it into a French-Italian dialect.

The book was completed in 1298. It was called *Divisament dou Monde* (Description of the World). Astounding, entertaining, and richly informative, it caused a sensation. By the time Polo died, his *Travels* had been translated into half a dozen languages. Its popularity was unprecedented in the Middle Ages. Polo was released from prison in 1299. He spent the rest of his life as a modestly successful merchant in his native Venice.

Marco Polo's *Travels* introduced Europeans to the huge continent of Asia. It told of an extensive Eastern civilization almost entirely unknown to them, one far in advance of their own. Many found Polo's stories too fantastic to be true, and his credibility was attacked. How could the barbaric Mongols possibly be living in safety, comfort, and luxury at the farthest edge of the world? According to one famous legend, even family and friends of the Polos did not believe his claims. They were persuaded of their truth only after the travelers ripped open the seams of their clothes and precious gems poured out. On his deathbed, Marco Polo was asked to admit his Chinese tales were not true. He replied, "I did not write half of what I saw."

The *Travels* does contain errors. Polo relied on secondhand information for some of the book. Other parts were based on travelers' legends. One such account of the mythical Christian Asian kingdom of Prester

In service to Kublai Khan, Marco, Niccoló, and Maffeo traveled all over Asia. According to Marco's book, the Polos had asked permission to leave several times, but the khan liked them so much he refused to allow them to leave. They were finally able to leave in 1290, reaching Venice in 1295.

PRESTER JOHN

The history of exploration is marked by many expeditions and pursuits of mythical, legendary, or nonexistent places or people—Atlantis, Antilia, the Seven Cities of Cíbola, El Dorado. One of the more intriguing of such searches was for a figure once widely known to educated Westerners but now consigned to the footnotes of scholarly books—Prester John.

His very name, Prester, a version of "priest," hints at his reputation. Prester John was said to be a Christian priest who supposedly ruled a fabulously wealthy kingdom far from the known Christian world. The first written account of Prester John appeared in Europe in 1145. It described his kingdom as somewhere at the far edges of central Asia. The image of Prester John as a powerful ruler was reinforced in 1165 when a letter supposedly written by John was found. In it, John called himself king of the Three Indies. He claimed his army consisted of 140,000 cavalrymen and 100,000 infantrymen. The letter was not genuine, but many people believed it was. It was translated into a number of languages and read throughout Europe with great excitement.

European monarchs, embroiled in the Crusades, saw in Prester John a potentially valuable ally against the Muslims. In 1177, the Roman Catholic pope Alexander III sent an envoy out to look for him. He was never heard of again. Medieval European travelers from about 1200 on, including Marco Polo, searched for and wrote about Prester John, only now the kingdom tended to be located in northern India or the Caucasus region of southwest Asia and southeast Europe. Although such claims were little more than rumors, they kept the story alive.

By the 1300s, Prester John's kingdom was believed to be in Africa and the quest was revived with a new intensity. In the 1400s, that search was largely conducted by Portuguese explorers sailing for Prince Henry the Navigator and then the king of Portugal, John (João) II. Some of these explorers sought Prester John's kingdom in Ethiopia. Others looked along the coast of western Africa. No expedition ever found such a man or kingdom.

John, which Polo describes as if it was real. In many passages Rustichello exaggerated the facts for literary effect. In addition, other vital information was left out, too. *Travels* fails to mention chopsticks, the Chinese practice of foot-binding, or the striking ideographic (symbol-based) Chinese script. Many commentators over the years have noted that Marco Polo also left out the Great Wall. Most of the information in the *Travels* has, however, been confirmed by documentary evidence. Polo, according to modern scholars, is usually a reliable reporter.

Polo's *Travels* was one of the most influential books of the Middle Ages. Europeans were excited by his account of the fabulous riches to be found in the Far East. They longed for Asian rubies, pearls, pepper, cloves, silks and porcelain. All of these luxury items could make traders' fortunes. Best of all, Polo's book outlined the routes that led to their source.

Hostile Islamic kingdoms that succeeded the Mongol Empire along the Silk Roads in central Asia barred Westerners from retracing the Polos' footsteps along the overland routes. Instead, Portuguese, Spanish, Dutch, and English sailors looked for a sea route around Africa to Asia. They did not succeed until the late fifteenth century.

The Polos had journeyed to China during a brief window in which medieval Europeans and Asians enjoyed free contact. Marco Polo's *Travels* stood as a definitive European reference to Asia for 200 years. In the late fifteenth century, Christopher Columbus carefully annotated his copy. The sixteenth-century English explorer Martin Frobisher read it, too. The *Travels* was an outstanding work of medieval geography and anthropology. It is still the best contemporary source of information about Mongol court life. The marvels of medieval Chinese society that Marco Polo described more than 700 years ago still surprise and awe Western readers.

8

Mysteries, Legends, and Lies

CLEARLY, MANY INDIVIDUALS DID TRAVEL DURING THE MIDDLE Ages. However, most people had neither the means, the opportunity, nor the courage to travel. Instead, they stayed close to home. They enjoyed the tales brought back by pilgrims, traders, soldiers, and explorers. Travelers' tales of exotic humans, creatures, and places had circulated for centuries by the time of the Middle Ages. Medieval literature is rich in histories, geographies, itineraries, guidebooks, phrasebooks, real and fictional descriptions of journeys, and letters from travelers.

It is important to remember that the medieval world was very different from the modern world. The knowledge and writings of scholars were restricted to a small religious and political elite. Most people, including the explorers, were uneducated. Facts were scarce, and superstitions abounded.

Travelers and writers often lied about their experiences. Other false reports came from simple mistakes. Sometimes travelers' accounts only existed by word-of-mouth for centuries before being written down. Even then, in an age before the invention of printing, manuscripts were written and copied by hand, and errors were inevitably introduced.

There was a lot that people did not know, so they filled in the blanks with fantastic landscapes and monsters. Travelers regularly told of meeting humans with only one eye or one huge foot, or with tails, two heads, or no heads at all. Even Marco Polo described people with dogs' heads, a mountain stream gushing diamonds, and a desert populated by ghouls. Travelers' accounts commonly depicted unfamiliar regions

Monsters and mythical creatures often appeared in manuscripts, church carvings, and other cultural artifacts. Above is a picture of fish and fantastical creatures from a thirteenth-century manuscript.

as paradises. These distant lands stood in contrast to the daily reality of poverty, plagues, famines, and political turmoil. Most people had every reason to believe that monstrous races of people, cannibals, mermaids, and earthly paradises were real.

Legendary and mythical places found their way onto maps and stayed there. Explorers sometimes claimed to have discovered a legendary island. Mapmakers would often add it in the "correct," newly reported spot but neglect to remove it from its previous hypothetical location. In 1443, the Portuguese regent, Dom Pedro, brother of Prince Henry the Navigator, complained about these maps. He ranted that unknown regions were shown on maps "according to the pleasure of the men who made them" instead of being based on observation. Imaginative maps occasionally inspired valuable expeditions, however. In the fifteenth century, Portuguese explorers mapped the West African coast while they were searching for a mythical river of gold.

MEDIEVAL MONSTERS

Most Europeans of the early Middle Ages knew little about distant lands. Faraway lands were thought to be uninhabitable or occupied by monsters. These monsters took a number of forms. Some were serpents or monkeys. Others were dragons, unicorns, or griffins. (Griffins had a lion's body and claws and an eagle's wings and beak.)

There were animal-human hybrids, too. Stories tell of mermaids, human bodies with goats' feet or dogs' heads, and lions' or locusts' bodies with human heads. People living in distant lands were described as horribly deformed. Some had their faces on their chests. Others had a single large foot that they raised over their heads like umbrellas or huge flapping ears that served as pillows, blankets, or wings.

Throughout the European Middle Ages, thousands of monsters appeared in books, church carvings and stained glass windows, maps, and travelers' tales. Illustrated encyclopedias of animals included mythical and monstrous ones. The monsters represented evil, moral corruption, barbarians, and non-Christians.

Some Christian clerics objected to the large number of monsters. In the 1120s, St. Bernard of Clairvaux attacked the widespread intrusion of monsters into monastic settings: "What excuse can there be for these ridiculous monstrosities in the cloisters where the monks do their reading, extraordinary things at once beautiful and ugly?" Bernard's complaint answered its own question. Monsters were enjoyably scary in the Middle Ages. In different forms—such as aliens, predatory sharks, giant gorillas, and dinosaurs—they remain so today.

It is clear, then, that many false beliefs, errors, and outright lies emerged during the Middle Ages. Some have survived to the present day. All who want to understand the true history of exploration must weigh the evidence and decide which claims have merit.

ST. BRENDAN'S VOYAGE

One of the most popular travel stories of the Middle Ages told of a voyage by the Irish Christian monk St. Brendan. Born in about A.D. 484, Brendan founded monasteries in Ireland and Scotland. It is likely he traveled as far as Wales and northwestern France. Legends tell of two additional voyages he made. Both were to the island known as the Land of Promise of the Saints. It was also called the Promised Land, or Promised Isles. This was the Christian paradise.

Brendan's first voyage was unsuccessful. On the second, lasting from A.D. 565 to 573, he was said to have reached the island. The *Voyage of St. Brendan*, written down in the ninth century, claimed to be based on Brendan's own telling of "everything he remembered of the voyage." Having received directions from the venerable abbot Barinth, who had already visited the Promised Land, Brendan and 14 companions built a coracle, or curragh. This small, lightweight vessel of wicker or light wood was covered with animal hide and waterproofed with tallow. The men stowed spare hides, tools, and food for 40 days. They set off, heading "toward the summer solstice."

According to the *Voyage*, Brendan spent seven years at sea. He traveled among many Atlantic islands trying to reach the Promised Land. He encounters devils, sea monsters, sheep as large as bulls, and huge white birds. These birds are fallen angels that sing Christian psalms and speak to Brendan in perfect Latin. Once having put ashore on a barren black island and made a cooking fire, the land suddenly slips under the water. The "island" was actually a whale. The whale tells them they can camp on him as long as they do not light any more fires on his back. Eventually Brendan and his companions come to an island covered with apple trees and springs. They have reached the Promised Land. There a young man greets them, saying,

Now, at last, you have found the land you have been seeking all these years. The Lord Jesus Christ did not allow you to find it

immediately, because first He wished to show you the richness of His wonders in the deep.

The *Voyage* was accepted as truth. "Brendan's Island" subsequently appeared on European maps for centuries, located in the Atlantic off northwestern Africa. Sometimes it was placed near the Canary Islands or Madeira. Often it was located near the legendary island of Antilia. By the late fifteenth century, the island was reported to have been sighted in the Azores. Even Christopher Columbus recorded in his diary that he had heard of its exact position.

Some people have even suggested that Brendan visited North America. A sixteenth-century map locates "San Brandan Island" off Newfoundland, Canada. Generations of European mariners searched the Atlantic Ocean for it. The last such expedition sailed in 1721. Not until 1759 was the Land of Promise of the Saints finally recognized as mythological.

No evidence has ever supported the idea that Brendan sailed to the eastern Atlantic Ocean or to North America. Brendan was, however, a historical figure. Many scholars believe that the ideas behind the *Voyage to the Promised Land* came from actual voyages. The "curdled" sea he described was likely ice. He may have visited the Shetlands, the Faeroe Islands, and Iceland. Such voyages were possible in the sixth century, and they would account for the volcanoes, waterfalls, and icebergs described in the story. Whether Brendan sailed so far, however, cannot now be known.

MANY ATLANTIC ISLANDS

In 1558, the Venetian Nicolò Zeno published *The Discovery of the Ilands Frislanda . . . Estotilanda and Icaria, by Two Zeni Brothers.* It described the exploration of the western Atlantic by ancestors of Nicolò and Antonio Zeno in about 1380. The book was supposedly based on their letters. Shipwrecked on an island called Frisland, they set sail again. This time they were joined by the Frislandian prince Zichmni. Together they visit the islands of Estotiland, whose people understand Latin, and Drogeo. There, the people "feed upon man's flesh, as the sweetest meat in their judgment there is." A third stop is a land rich with gold and dotted with castles. Its people practice human sacrifice.

The book included a map showing all these islands, which in due course, made their way onto European maps. Some people have since identified Frisland as the Faeroe Islands. Others think the Zenos reached eastern Canada. Estotiland is Labrador, they say, and Drogeo is Newfoundland.

This legend was further complicated in the eighteenth century by the identification of Prince Zichmni as Henry Sinclair, earl of Orkney and Caithness. He died around 1400. Some of Sinclair's descendants claim that Sinclair himself landed on Nova Scotia, Canada, in 1398 and in Massachusetts in 1399. In any case, scholars have exposed the Zeno book as fiction. The Zeno brothers did not discover new islands, nor did they reach North America. The text is pieced together from information about other explorers' expeditions to the Americas. The map combines features of the Faeroe Islands and Iceland. One of Nicolò Zeno's motives in writing the false account seems to have been family pride. He also wanted to restore the reputation of Venice as a great maritime power.

During the later Middle Ages, the islands of the Atlantic Ocean became an attraction for Mediterranean seafarers long locked into their inland sea by the treacherous Straits of Gibraltar between Spain and North Africa. New oceangoing vessels and navigational aids opened the Atlantic to sailors. Real and imaginary voyages and islands multiplied.

The great twelfth-century Arab geographer al-Idrisi told of eight Muslim sailors who took on the Atlantic, which they called "the Sea of Perpetual Gloom." For 37 grueling days they survived treacherous seas, dangerous shallows, and human-eating monsters and other terrors before landing on the "Island of Sheep." (This land was most likely Madeira.) They then sailed onward to the Canary Islands. In time they reached the coast of Morocco in North Africa. In the course of this voyage, they allegedly discovered 30,000 islands. Like St. Brendan's *Voyage,* this account seems to be based on an actual voyage.

In 1424, the Venetian cartographer Zuane Pizzigano drew a nautical chart. It showed a new island called Antilia. It was a squarish island nearly as large as Ireland, and it lay in the Atlantic to the west of Europe. Antilia appeared on numerous later maps, shown sometimes as a large island and other times as a continent or archipelago.

Antilia was tied to an old legend of the founding of seven Christian cities on an Atlantic island. In the story, a Christian archbishop, six bishops, and their followers fled from the Moors (North African Muslims). They first crossed Spain and Portugal, and then sailed westward far into the Atlantic. The group eventually reached an island, where they built seven cities where they lived peacefully ever after. The island became known as the Island of the Seven Cities. The first terrestrial globe ever made, in 1492, includes a note telling a similar story. It states that "in 1414 a ship from Spain got nearest to [Antilia] without danger."

Antilia joined a group of supposed islands that drew sailors farther and farther into the Atlantic in search of them. In the sixteenth century, the Spanish historian Bartolomé de Las Casas wrote of an accidental Portuguese landfall on Antilia 100 years earlier:

> *A storm-driven ship landed at the Isle of Seven Cities in the time of the Infante D[om] Henrique [Prince Henry the Navigator]. The crew was welcomed by the natives in good Portuguese and urged*

Christopher Columbus and other explorers went in search of Antilia, an imaginary group of islands in the Atlantic. Columbus believed he had found Antilia when he first landed on islands in the Caribbean. They later became known as the Antilles (*above*).

to remain, but declined. On the way home they found grains of gold in the sand that they had taken in for their cook-box. When they reported this to the Infante, he scolded them for not procuring more information, and ordered them to return, which they refused to do.

This Portuguese crew was frightened of the island's magic. Others were not. On June 25, 1474, the Florentine scientist Paolo Toscanelli sent a map to Afonso V, king of Portugal. He thought it was possible to reach Asia by sailing west. His map showed Antilia in the Atlantic Ocean halfway between Portugal and Japan. In a letter, he wrote, "From the Island of Antilia, which you call the Seven Cities, to the most noble island of Cipangu [Japan] it is 50 degrees of longitude, in other words 2,500 miles [4,023 km]." Christopher Columbus expected to find Antilia on his first transatlantic voyage (1492). Many of his crew members believed they had located it, and the West Indies were thenceforth known as the Antilles.

Antilia never existed, yet it appeared on maps throughout the sixteenth century. The legend of the Seven Cities lived on in the Seven Golden Cities of Cíbola. These were legendary cities sought by the Spanish conquistadores in North America.

Hy-Brasil was another mythical Atlantic island. In the Irish language, Gaelic, the name means "isle of the blessed." Belonging to Irish legend, in its earliest form perhaps from the pre-Christian era, accounts of this island were influenced by several early medieval Irish seafaring myths. In *The Adventure of Bran, Son of Febal*, first written down in the seventh century, Bran travels to Hy-Brasil. It is a paradise supported on golden pillars. No one is ever sad or ill there. They are always happy, continually playing games to music. Like many mythical islands, this one was constantly hidden in mist and cloud. Every seven years the clouds parted and the island became visible. By 1325, Hy-Brasil appeared on a map drawn by Angelo Dalorto. On later maps, it was often called "Brasil Rock." Usually located west of Ireland, the island is shown closer to North America on later maps. Some charts show a second Brasil in the Azores.

In 1452, Portuguese prince Henry the Navigator sent Diogo de Tieve to find Hy-Brasil. De Tieve failed, although he did find two islands in the Azores. In 1480, John Lloyd led the first of many expeditions to locate Hy-Brasil. He sailed in circles for nine weeks and came home empty-handed.

Hy-Brasil remained on British maps until 1873. As recently as 1912, T.J. Westropp published an article in the journal of the Royal Irish Academy claiming that he had seen this island three times. He described his last sighting in 1872, on "a clear evening, with a fine golden sunset, when just as the sun went down, a dark island suddenly appeared far out to sea, but not on the horizon. It had two hills, one wooded; between these, from a low plain, rose towers and curls of smoke." His companions, including his mother, saw it too. Despite their claims, Hy-Brasil is purely mythical. There is no evidence at all for its existence.

ENCOUNTERING THE AMERICAS

Today, a steady market exists for books "proving" ancient European, African, or Asian knowledge of the Americas, offering supposed evidence of foreign influence on various Native American cultures. Arguments have been made for pre-Columbian contacts with the Americas by everyone from ancient Phoenicians to the Welsh, Africans, and Chinese. No evidence exists to prove that any of them reached the Americas, but a few of the major contenders deserve attention.

Leif Eriksson is now widely accepted to have made the first European landfall in the Americas in about A.D. 1000. He opened a very brief period of attempted colonization. Some people believe, however, that the Viking presence was more widespread and of much longer duration. More than 30 rocks with alleged runic inscriptions (runes are the script used in writing medieval Norse languages) were offered as evidence.

In 1898, an inscribed stone was found by a farmer near Kensington, Minnesota. Its inscriptions were translated:

> *8 Goths [Swedes] and 22 Norwegians on a voyage of discovery from Vinland westward. We had our camp by 2 skerries [rocky islets] one day's journey north of this stone. . . . We have 10 men by the sea to look after our ships. . . . Year 1362.*

This stone was cited as proof that the Vikings had visited the interior of North America. Most scholars believe it is a nineteenth-century fake. The other rocks include a boulder at No Man's Island near Martha's

Vineyard, Massachusetts. Its runes spell Leif Eriksson's name. This one is a twentieth-century hoax. A stone in Heavener, Oklahoma, contains an inscription translated as "GNOMENDAL." This supposedly represents a Viking's first initial and last name. Scholars reject all claims that it is genuine.

Other evidence for a Norse presence in North America has also been dismissed by scholars. Local people and tourist authorities may still point them out with pride. The "Viking fort" in Newport, Rhode Island, was actually a tower built by English colonists in the seventeenth century. A number of so-called Viking mooring holes were found along the Atlantic coast and as far west as Minnesota. They were in fact drilled by much later sailors.

The Norse saga of Erik the Red relates that after the Vikings began to settle Ireland in the ninth century, the Irish fled to Greenland or Newfoundland. However, no evidence supporting this claim has been found in North America, and the case for a medieval Irish encounter with the New World remains unproven.

One of the most popular of the early European discoveries of the Americas is the story of Prince Madoc of Wales. It was first published in England in 1583 as "a true report." Madoc was said to have sailed in 1170 and found a site for settlement near present-day Mobile, Alabama. He left 120 companions there, then sailed back to Wales, returning later with 10 more ships carrying colonists. These Welsh immigrants allegedly disappeared up the Alabama River and became a Native American tribe. Over time, the Welsh were linked with 20 different Native American peoples.

The languages of the Native American peoples, it was claimed, contained Welsh words. The Reverend Morgan Jones claimed to have preached in Welsh in 1669 to a tribe in the Carolinas. He claims he was understood. Information about the "Welsh" North American tribe was included as fact in U.S. history textbooks in the nineteenth century. In 1953, the Daughters of the American Revolution erected a monument at Fort Morgan in Mobile Bay, Alabama, with the inscription, "In memory of Prince Madoc, a Welsh explorer, who landed on the shores of Mobile Bay in 1170, and left behind, with the Indians, the Welsh language." There is no evidence that any Native American language is related to Welsh, and Madoc himself existed only in legend.

Some scholars claimed that sub-Saharan Africans visited the Americas long before Columbus. One Arabic source records that Abu Bakari II, "Voyager King" of the great empire of Mali in West Africa, sponsored two expeditions to South America. The voyages supposedly took place between 1305 and 1312. On the first voyage, 200 canoes crossed the Atlantic and landed in Brazil. Only three returned. Abu Bakari led the second expedition himself. This story and others like it are controversial. This field continues to be a lively area of historical research.

The merchants of Bristol, England, also have their champions. Bristol's sailors were trading in Iceland in the early 1400s. They had the best navigational technology and nautical skills in Europe. During the winter of 1497–1498, the English merchant John Day wrote a letter, almost certainly addressed to Christopher Columbus. The letter stated that sailors from Bristol had already reached North America. Day also claimed that they had also discovered Hy-Brasil. He even supplies the latitude of the Isle of the Seven Cities. No other evidence for these feats exists, however. Most scholars do not believe that the English traders of Bristol reached North America before Columbus.

There are tales that claim people from the Iberian Peninsula were founders of the New England kingdom of Iargalon ("land beyond the sunset") in about 1000 B.C. Other "evidence" links ancient Phoenicians with American sites. Egyptian astronomer-priests supposedly built temple-mounds in Central America. Islamic texts tell of Muslim sailors reaching the Americas in the ninth, tenth, and thirteenth centuries. Supporters of these claims point to Arabic words in rock inscriptions and Native American place-names. Serious scholarship has rejected all these claims.

Many people of the Middle Ages understood that the known world was expanding. However, they could not be sure of the details. The discoveries of real explorers inevitably became garbled through oral transmission. True accounts were joined by myths and exaggerated into legends. Firsthand accounts, maps, exotic artifacts, and wishful thinking all contributed to the mix. They produced imaginative travel literature. Most of the stories' claims can be explained or dismissed. Even so, reading them can still stimulate careful thought and provide great pleasure.

9

Portugal's Master Sailors

FROM CLASSICAL TIMES TO THE LATE MIDDLE AGES, PORTUGAL has played a supporting role in its own history, secondary only to the foreigners—Romans, Visigoths, Muslims, and the Spanish—who have controlled the Iberian peninsula. Portugal became independent from Spain in 1143, but it was not until 1385 that Portugal was fully free from Spain. The next year, King John I of Portugal married Philippa of Lancaster. She was half-sister of the future King Henry IV of England. Their marriage created a bond between the English and the Portuguese. The king was eventually known as King John the Great because he stabilized Portugal and started it on the way to become one of the most powerful states in Europe.

John's five children were well educated. Duarte, the oldest boy, was trained to succeed his father as king. All the other children developed special skills. The third-oldest son was Henry. His special interest is indicated by the name history has given him: Henry the Navigator.

EXPLORING THE AFRICAN COAST

Prince Henry's first goal was to map the western coast of Africa. Then, after the southern tip of Africa had been rounded, he planned to establish the sea route to India and beyond. The results of exploration would include exotic trade goods and wealth. For Henry, another reward would be the thrill of discovery.

Henry sent voyages of exploration south from the Portuguese Sagres to the northwest corner of Africa. At the time, Europeans knew almost nothing of the west coast of Africa. Cape Não (No) in Morocco was the farthest south any European had ever gone.

> If you round Cape No
> You may return or no.

Portuguese prince Henry the Navigator (*left*) wanted to find the sea route to India and the East via the southern tip of Africa. He is believed to have founded a school for navigators and mapmakers and supported the best mariners in their expeditions.

Sailors knew of and believed in this saying. Still, Henry was determined that his sailors continue farther south. He believed the shoreline would swing away to the east, indicating that the continent of Africa had been rounded. India would lie ahead. Sometime in 1417 or 1418, Henry sent a reluctant crew to round Cape Não. They found no sea monsters. They did not find an ocean boiling with deadly heat. Both of these things had been predicted.

Year after year, Henry sent out ships that made important discoveries along the long Moroccan coast. In 1434, Gil Eannes rounded Cape Bojador (in modern-day Western Sahara), 200 miles (321.8 km) south of Cape Não. In 1441, Nuño Tristão reached a bulge in northwest Africa at about 21° north latitude. He named it Cape Branco. Tristão brought home African captives from the voyage, initiating the African slave trade. The Portuguese were a part of the slave trade for the rest of the exploration period. Slavery had been widely practiced for centuries. Europeans enslaved other Europeans. Africans enslaved other Africans. Henry and his captains saw nothing wrong in capturing and selling African slaves. As they saw it, they were obtaining cheap labor. They also thought they were saving heathen souls.

By 1442, Portuguese voyages to Africa had become routine. As the explorers began to encounter desert nomads and slaves and tribespeople from the African interior, a small trickle of gold dust began to return to Portugal. In exchange, the Portuguese traded brightly colored clothing, utensils, and gaudy trinkets. The gold came from Guinea, far to the south. It was a land of plentiful water and green forests, and the Portuguese hoped that a river of gold flowed through Guinea from the fabled kingdom of Christian king Prester John. So it was with great optimism that Henry, in 1442, set his sights on reaching Guinea.

In 1443, Tristão was sent south to explore beyond Cape Branco with a single ship. Seventy-five miles (120.7 km) south of that cape (in present-day Mauritania) he found a calm and well-protected bay that contained a number of small islands. In time, the bay, the largest island, and the Portuguese settlement that grew there were named Arguin. Tristão captured as many native people as his ship would hold and returned to Sagres.

In 1455, a young captain from Venice named Alvise da Cadamosto sailed out of the Mediterranean Sea bound for Flanders (Belgium), in search of trading opportunities and adventure. Blown off course, he landed at Lagos, Portugal, a maritime town near Sagres where Henry built his ships. Henry was impressed by the character and trading experience of the young man and agreed to provide him with a cargo for trading along the African coast, hoping that he would voyage as far as Guinea. In 1455, Cadamosto left Lagos, picking up provisions, as was customary, at Porto Santo (Madeira) and at the Canaries. He was joined by another ship captained by Italian Antoniotto Usodimare of Genoa. Cadamosto reached the Gambia River and sailed inland, hoping to find friendly native people with whom he could trade. Instead, four miles (6.4 km) upriver, the exploring party was attacked by 15 boatloads of warriors. The Europeans barely escaped with their lives. At the urging of their crews, Cadamosto and Usodimare returned to Portugal.

The great shoulder of West Africa had been rounded. Existing maps showed that the southern tip of Africa was close, and then India and the East would lie ahead. But in fact, the huge, unexplored mass of southern Africa still lay ahead. It stretched another 1,000 miles (1,609.3 km) south before the shoreline would turn to the east. Cadamosto had not even come close to reaching the equator. Had Prince Henry understood the difficulties of his quest he might not have persevered. But in 1456, he told Cadamosto to go farther south.

Cadamosto sailed south as far as Cape Branco, where the expedition was blown off-course by a violent storm. Far off shore, the sailors were surprised to see a group of five islands, all uninhabited by humans but teeming with tame birds in a lush pleasant setting. Cadamosto claimed them for Portugal and named them the Cape Verde Islands. Although several Europeans had visited these islands before him, Cadamosto would continue to insist he had discovered them.

Cadamosto then sailed back east to the mainland and once again sailed up the Gambia River. This time he met no hostility from the African peoples. A lively trade developed in the Gambian interior. In exchange for his goods, Cadamosto received a bit of gold dust. He also got civet cats, baboons, marmots, and tropical fruit. The Europeans saw bizarre things they had never heard of or seen before. Cadamosto described the hippopotamus (he called it the horse-fish). He wrote about giant bats, strange birds, and unusual varieties of fish. Wild elephants roamed about, hunted by the native peoples and killed with poison arrows for their meat and their ivory tusks.

Cadamosto left the interior of Gambia and sailed farther south. His men were ill with fever, scurvy, and the terrible heat. The ships landed 150 miles (241.4 km) south of the Gambia River at Bissagos Island (in present-day Guinea-Bissau). Friendly native people welcomed the travelers but the two groups could not understand a word of the others' language, creating difficulties in trading. Cadamosto returned to Portugal with his feverish crew. The expedition had not brought back much cargo, but it had claimed new lands for Portugal. In addition, the men had sailed farther south than any previous explorers and also learned a lot about the interior of Africa.

PRINCE HENRY'S ROLE IN EXPLORATION

In 1415, King John I of Portugal successfully attacked and took the Moorish city of Ceuta, a major trading post in Morocco, across the strait from the Spanish city of Gibraltar. Prince Henry was knighted by his father on the day of victory and was named governor of the territory of Algarve (southern Portugal). With these honors came a huge fortune and Henry retired to Sagres (on Cape St. Vincent, the southwest corner of Portugal). There he founded an "institute of exploration" devoted to the study of navigation and exploration. He invited some of the best mathematicians and astronomers in Europe to join him. Henry set these men to work in his school of navigation, drawing up charts and maps. This elite group refined all the existing tools of navigation. Henry also collected the best boat builders he could find to improve his ships to be used for expeditions. He then hired the best sailors in the kingdom and beyond.

Henry the Navigator's goal was to find the sea route to India and the Far East by sailing around the southern tip of Africa. Henry died in 1460 before this route had been discovered. However, there was hardly an early fifteenth-century Portuguese sailor or an expedition that he did not sponsor or inspire. Few people have the boldness, imagination, and simple good luck to put such a project as Henry's into operation. Even more extraordinary is the fact that a single person could affect the future of Europe, Africa, and Asia.

In 1457, Diogo Gomes, a good friend of Prince Henry, was ordered to lead an expedition as far south as possible. Gomes reached Bissagos Island but found the ocean currents so dangerous that he turned back. He retreated to the Gambia River and sailed upstream as far as his big ship could go. He was entertained by a native king who told him about the caravans that crossed the African desert. They came from Egypt in search of gold from the African interior. Gomes could not learn much more, as fever and sickness were overcoming him and his crew. He sailed for home.

THE PORTUGUESE PUSH ON

After Prince Henry died in 1460, his nephew King Afonso V of Portugal delegated the West African trade to Fernão Gomes (no relation to Diogo Gomes). Gomes was an entrepreneur and ship owner. He was ordered to explore 300 miles (482.2 km) of uncharted African coast every year. In 1471, Gomes arrived along the coast of present-day Ghana. There, he set up a trading post later to be known as the great gold-producing city of São Jorge de Mina (present-day Elmina). In the same year, he reached an island he named Fernando Po (now called Bioko) in the Gulf of Guinea. He was dismayed to find that the coastline turned sharply to the south; this meant that all the existing world maps available to the Portuguese were wrong, and no one knew how much farther south he would have to sail before he could round the tip of Africa. In 1473, Gomes sailed across the equator, but the next year the king relieved him of his commission.

Afonso V died in 1481. He was succeeded by his son, John II. One of John's first acts was to restore Portuguese sovereignty over the African trade. King John II sent heavily armed ships south to eliminate piracy within his territory. At home, he had the counting house for incoming cargo moved from Lagos to Lisbon, Portugal's capital. He wanted to look out his palace windows and watch the loads of gold, ivory, pepper, and other spices as they arrived from Africa.

King John II realized the post established by Fernão Gomes, Elmina, Ghana, was important because of its location close to the gold fields in Guinea. A fleet of warships and cargo ships was sent there to build a fort, under the direction of Diogo de Azambuja. This expedition was aided by the skill of Bartolomeu Dias, one of the ship captains. Soon gold was flowing from Elmina to Lisbon.

John II hoped to expand the Portuguese kingdom through exploration and exploitation. Gone was the bustling hub of navigation Henry had sponsored in Sagres. In its place was an organization in Lisbon of pilots, navigators, cosmographers, geographers and mapmakers who were anxious to continue the work begun by Henry. People began talking about seeking a western passage to India and the Far East, but John was not interested. In 1483, in fact, he rejected a brash young Italian named Christopher Columbus, who was seeking sponsorship for a western voyage to Asia.

In 1482, John appointed Diego Cão to command the next West African expedition. Cão left Portugal in April, rounded the bulge of West

Beginning with the expeditions of Prince Henry the Navigator, the Portuguese explored the west coast of Africa. Diego Cão explored the Congo River, the first European to do so. Today, the Congo River is a lifeline for millions of people, who depend on it for transportation and trade. Above, a man steers his canoe on the Congo River in order to sell bananas to passing boats.

Africa, and crossed the equator, landing at Cape Santa Catarina (in present-day Gabon). Steering due south and overcoming powerful tides and adverse currents, Cão became the first European to reach the mighty Congo (Zaire) River. He erected a large stone marker to record his arrival and established a Portuguese trading relationship with the Bakongo kingdom there. Cão pressed southward, reaching Cape Santa Maria Benguela (in present-day Angola) before returning home in 1484. He had sailed farther south than any European before him. The greatest achievement of this expedition, however, was his exploration of the Congo.

Cão led a second African expedition in 1485. On this voyage he further explored the Congo River, apparently navigating as far upriver as Yelala Falls. Once again, he sailed farther south than any other explorer; this time he reached Cape Cross (in present-day Namibia). Here, too, he put up a stone marker. It was eight feet (2.4 m) tall and weighed half a ton (453.5 kilograms). It read:

> *In the year of the World 6681, and the year 1482 after the birth of the Lord Jesus Christ, at the command of the glorious, most powerful and excellent King John II of Portugal, this country was discovered and this cross erected by Diego Cão, a knight at his court.*

Cão probably died on the return voyage in 1486. He had opened up the West African coast. Portuguese sailors were within striking distance of the southern tip of Africa. Beyond it lay the lucrative Indian Ocean trade.

In 1487, King John II planned an expedition that would, without fail, round the tip of Africa. Two 50-ton (45,359.2 kg) ships would make the voyage. A smaller supply ship would wait somewhere along the coast with supplies for the return trip. Bartolomeu Dias was in charge.

The expedition left Lisbon in August 1487. As they proceeded south, the explorers set up stone crosses at important points and assigned names to rivers and other geographical features. Just below the Tropic of Capricorn, fierce winds forced the ships to change direction back and forth for five days. Another horrific storm lasted for weeks and blew the expedition off course. When the seas calmed, the sailors realized that they had rounded Africa's southernmost tip. The ships followed the coast northward as far as the Rio do Iffante (Great Fish River). They were now off the southeast coast of present-day South Africa. By this point, the crew had had enough and they insisted on returning to Portugal. On the return voyage, the explorers landed on the cape, which Dias name Cabo Tormentoso or "cape of storms." It was soon renamed the Cape of Good Hope.

Dias returned to Lisbon. He had sailed 1,500 miles (2,414 km) farther south than any other European and had rounded the southern tip of Africa. The route to India was now open. In October 1495, John II died. He was succeeded by his queen's brother, Manuel I. Manuel was determined to control all trade with India, using force if necessary. Manuel planned to move the spice trade from the overland-and-Mediterranean route to the Portuguese sea route around Africa.

VASCO DA GAMA SAILS FOR THE EAST

Manuel I chose Vasco da Gama to start direct trading between Lisbon and the East. Da Gama was given four ships. All the ships were well armed and carried the most advanced navigational instruments and the latest maps. In the evening of July 8, 1497, all the officers and crew were taken by da Gama to a chapel and there they prayed together. They were forgiven of all sins in case they died on the voyage.

The ships sailed south, stopping at St. Helena Bay in November 1497. They were just short of the Cape of Good Hope. The sailors repaired their ships and took on water and food. Relations with the native people started out well, but soon the two sides fought. In the battle, da Gama was hit with an arrow. Here, and on many future occasions, da Gama's quick temper resulted in friendly beginnings ending in hostility.

The Portuguese rounded the cape and sailed north. The ships arrived at Mozambique along Africa's southeast coast by February. Here, da Gama met with Arab sheiks and Muslim traders, but these meetings ended badly. By means of extortion and torture of informants, da Gama obtained the services of an excellent guide who led him across the Indian Ocean to the coast of India. Within one year of leaving Portugal, da Gama arrived at Calicut. It was known as the richest of all the cities in India.

Da Gama's mission was supposed to set up peaceful trade relations. He was unable to accomplish this although the ruler of Calicut did send a letter to the king of Portugal urging trade between their two king-doms. Da Gama gained valuable information about the East, but his methods had instilled fear and anger, not respect, in all those he met. Nevertheless, a triumphant celebration was held for da Gama when he reached Lisbon in September 1499. He demanded and received extravagant rewards. The celebrated explorer married and settled comfortably into retirement. Very soon, however, he was asked to reenter the fray.

PORTUGAL SOLIDIFIES ITS POSITION

By 1500, everything was in place for the enrichment of Portugal. King Manuel knew where the riches were and how to get there, and he did not waste time. In March of that year, a 13-ship armada left Lisbon under the command of Pedro Álvars Cabral. The destination was Calicut, India. The purpose was trade.

The ships sailed south as usual via the Canary and Cape Verde Islands. After Cape Verde, the party took a wide swing to the west to avoid the equatorial doldrums. This region in the mid-Atlantic has flat, windless seas and sudden, violent storms. To their amazement, on April 22, the sailors sighted land to the west. Cabral had accidentally reached Brazil. Cabral claimed the new land for Portugal and sent word of its discovery back to King Manuel.

Upon landing, the Portuguese found peaceful inhabitants. A sailor on the voyage kept a diary. In it, he describes the Tupi Indians. He tells how they painted their eyelids and above the eyebrows with "figures of white and black and blue and red." They cut scars into their bodies and rubbed black pigment into them. Each scar recorded an enemy slain. Brave warriors were covered with scars. Cabral placed tin crucifixes around the necks of 60 new converts to Christianity. The next day, his ships continued on their way. They left behind a land bigger than the continent of Europe. It contained more riches than those of the East Indies for which Cabral was so eagerly bound.

At first the ships sped along on the winds, heading for the Cape of Good Hope. A violent storm hit them. After 20 days of furious winds and seas, only seven ships remained. The others had sunk with all hands. Another storm struck as they rounded the cape. One ship was blown off course and came upon a gigantic island. Thus by accident, like Brazil, Madagascar was "discovered" by the Europeans. The six remaining

A powerful reminder of Portugal's age of discovery, the Tower of Belem was built between 1515 and 1520 to commemorate Vasco da Gama and to defend Lisbon and its harbor. The last sight of departing Portuguese explorers and the first when they returned, the tower is now a United Nations Educational, Scientific and Cultural Organization (UNESCO) World Heritage Site.

ships went to Malindi, in present-day Kenya. It was the one city whose residents da Gama had not managed to alienate, and the Portuguese were welcomed there.

From Malindi, Cabral sailed to India. At first, trade in Calicut was friendly, but soon hostility erupted. A large number of Cabral's shore party were killed. One sailor described the terrible revenge exacted by Cabral. Ten ships owned by Muslim traders were taken. Their cargo was stolen and their ships were burned, and 500 or 600 men were killed. Nine unloaded ships were also burned, and three elephants were killed and eaten. The next day, the Portuguese ships drew up to the city and bombarded it. They killed "an endless number of people" and partially destroyed the city.

Cabral's ships then sailed 100 miles (160.9 km) south to the city of Cochin where, under the circumstances, the merchants were inclined to accommodate Cabral. Two weeks later the fleet sailed for home. Filled with treasure, they reached Lisbon in July 1501. Of the original 13 ships, only six returned. The wealth they contained more than made up for the losses.

Manuel's next move was designed to hold on to what he had gained. Da Gama came out of retirement to lead the next major expedition to India. He was seething at the attack on Cabral's men at Calicut. He also still held a grudge against the ruler of Calicut. Da Gama's 1502 voyage was not one of exploration. It was a voyage of revenge and conquest. Any city unwilling to trade with Portugal was in danger of being destroyed. Da Gama's ships were loaded with traded or looted goods. He was satisfied that he had laid the groundwork for Portuguese domination of a large region of the East.

As the sixteenth century began, the goals of King John I had been achieved. The visions for the future of Henry the Navigator had been realized. But the motivation to find, know, and map the unknown portions of the world was gone. Exploration had become a means to wealth and conquest. The riches it earned transformed Portugal into one of the wealthiest nations in the world.

10

The Dawning of the Age of Discovery

BY THE LATE FIFTEENTH CENTURY, THE MOST DYNAMIC OF THE world's civilizations were the Islamic world and western Europe. The rise of Islam created an enormous empire with a shared culture, causing the most striking political change in the medieval world. By the late Middle Ages, Islamic civilization led the world in learning and technology. Islamic scholars had a more complete and accurate understanding of world geography than any other people at the time.

During the Middle Ages, western Europe had seen wars, famines, and epidemics. The early medieval period was a time of decline in geographical knowledge—in fact, the term *geography* fell out of use. By the late fifteenth century, however, Europe's fortunes had improved. The rise of nation-states provided political stability, and trade created prosperity. The revival of classical learning built a class of well-educated people. The arts flourished. By the late Middle Ages, a handful of European states had become wealthy.

Travel accounts, like Marco Polo's, were read by many. They added to Europeans' geographical understanding. Hand-written books had been previously restricted to monastic scholars and the very wealthy, but the invention of the printing press in Europe in the late fifteenth century gave many people access to information. Ptolemy's *Geography*, for example, written in the second century A.D., was largely unknown in Europe until its publication in the fifteenth century. Ptolemy's system of longitude and latitude opened the possibility of long-distance navigation.

THE ROLE OF MAPS

After a long period of decline, European mapmaking finally began to improve in the late medieval period. The first scientifically prepared maps were coastal charts called *portolans*. They were developed in Italy and Spain in the thirteenth century. The artists who drew them added lines representing the compass directions, which were used for laying out accurate compass courses. There were also large, circular, more detailed religious maps. One such map that survives from the Middle Ages is the Hereford Mappamundi (ca. 1300). Drawn by an English priest named Richard of Haldingham (or Lafford), it shows real towns alongside biblical scenes and the Garden of Eden.

Johannes Gutenberg (*right*) is given credit as the first person to print a book, the Bible, with movable type in 1455. Here Gutenberg and his partner Johann Fust (*left*) hold the first proof from moveable type on the press they set up together.

Scientifically based world maps gradually replaced these religious models. Mapmakers made a serious attempt to include recent discoveries by navigators and travelers. However, they continued to include some information based on mythology, literature, and Christian teachings. The Catalan Atlas (1375) is the finest map produced during the European Middle Ages. Made by Cresques Abraham of Majorca, it included information from *portolans* and showed the West African coast beyond the point thus far reached by European mariners. It was the first map anywhere to show an accurate outline of India and Ceylon.

By the end of the Middle Ages, Europeans knew very accurately and in great detail the geography of their own continent, the entire Mediterranean, and the Black Sea. Recent Portuguese voyages had added the eastern Atlantic islands—Madeira, Majorca, the Canaries, and the Azores—to the known world. The coastline of West Africa had been filled in as far south as the Cape of Good Hope. The Europeans also understood the relative positions of eastern lands to China and the East Indies. They lacked accurate maps of distant regions, however. Throughout the Middle Ages, mapmakers relied on Marco Polo's *Travels*. Many were hampered by their belief that the Earth's hottest lands were uninhabitable.

THE LIMITATIONS OF OTHER PEOPLES

What had happened to China and India? At the beginning of the Middle Ages both of these civilizations had seemed ready to explore and expand. Toward the end of the period, however, China isolated itself. In the late 1400s, China was still a rich and advanced empire. Chinese admiral Zheng He's voyages had shown China's superb shipbuilding and seafaring skills, but after the admiral's final voyage in 1433, the Ming emperor had destroyed the imperial fleet. Navigating the open seas became a crime in China in the early sixteenth century. China yielded the rich East Indies trade to Arabs and Indians.

As for India, by the end of the Middle Ages it had exerted such a strong cultural influence regionally that a huge area encompassing India, Southeast Asia, and the East Indies was commonly referred to as "Greater India." India had created links from the Red Sea to Sumatra. However, the Indians restricted themselves to trade and showed no interest in pure exploration. In addition, the small states in South Asia seemed to always be at war. Finally, Hindu scholars were bound by tradition; they did not readily absorb innovation, discoveries, or foreign influences.

Like many peoples around the world in this time, most Native Americans were familiar only with their tribal regions. Even the great Aztec and Inca empires, both at their height in the fourteenth and fifteenth centuries, were essentially self-contained. Although the Aztec had mapped a large territory extending from present-day central Mexico to Honduras and knew virtually all of Central America, the absence of pack animals to carry food and water prevented them from undertaking long-distance travel. The Inca, occupying a 2,500-mile-long (4,023.3-km-long) region in South America from present-day Colombia to Chile, had thousands of miles of paved roads linking religious sites and settlements. But they, too, rarely strayed beyond the shrines and settlements in the interior of their empire. Both empires were confined by their limited technology. Their open boats, for example, were no match for the oceans, preventing them from traveling the open seas.

THE ACCOMPLISHMENTS OF MEDIEVAL EXPLORERS

What had medieval explorers discovered? Most achievements belonged to the seafarers. The Norse had visited North America. Along the way they had settled the major North Atlantic islands, from the Shetlands and Faeroes across to Iceland and Greenland. The Portuguese had discovered the islands of the East Atlantic, and Portuguese and Spanish colonists had settled them. Portuguese sailors had mapped the entire western African coast all the way to the Cape of Good Hope.

Chinese sailors had reached East Africa. In the Pacific, Polynesian sailors had explored and settled a huge region reaching from Hawaii to New Zealand. In about 1050, the Norseman Harald Hardrada had sailed through the Arctic Ocean and into the White Sea. These may seem like modest results for 1,000 years' worth of seafaring, but such long voyages into unknown waters were great achievements because they required advanced ships, sophisticated navigation, and sheer courage.

The world was still a patchwork of civilizations, but cultures separated by long distances were now in contact. Those primarily responsible were Arabic, Indian, and European merchants who were trading along overland and maritime routes. Their journeys had linked Europe, Africa, and Asia.

At the same time, thousands of Christian and Islamic pilgrims traveled to the Middle East. Christian missionaries reached central Asia, India, and China. Arab traders had also reached the East Indies and North African merchants crossed the Sahara Desert into the African interior. Chinese fleets called at the ports of India, Persia, Arabia, and East Africa. These contacts contributed to a slow but steady flow of information about geography, history, customs, religion, learning, technology, and innovation.

Fulcher (Foucher) of Chartres, France, a twelfth-century historian, was aware of a historic shift in consciousness. "In our time," he wrote,

> *God has transformed the Occident [West] into the Orient [East].*
> *For we who were Occidentals have now become Orientals. . . . We*
> *have already forgotten the places of our birth; already these are*
> *unknown to many of us or not mentioned any more. . . . He who*
> *was born a stranger is now as one born here; he who was born an*
> *alien has become a native.*

NEW CHALLENGES FOR EXPLORERS

As the end of the fifteenth century approached, several challenges for exploration loomed large. The enormous interiors of Asia and Africa were unknown by outsiders. Their remoteness and the difficulty of the terrain kept these continents from being fully explored until the nineteenth and twentieth centuries.

Explorers had yet to master the world's seas. Separated by oceans, people of the Eastern and Western hemispheres knew nothing of one another. No one knew the number or location of all the continents. The exact size of Earth was uncertain. During the Middle Ages, the Earth was generally agreed to be a sphere. What lay on the other side of the world and whether the Atlantic and Pacific oceans were fully navigable were mysteries, although a growing number of Europeans suspected that circumnavigation was possible.

During the Middle Ages, advances in shipbuilding technology helped the Europeans push farther and farther into the open sea. The ships of northern Europe became broader and deeper. Two new types of ship were developed. The cog had high sides, a deep draft, and a sternpost rudder. It was sturdy, maneuverable, and cheap to

THE SEARCH FOR SPICES

The search for spices is a recurring theme in the history of exploration. Why were spices so highly valued? Since at least classical Greek times, spices were luxuries in western Europe. They were used in cooking and for medicinal purposes. In Europe during the Middle Ages, black pepper was the seasoning most commonly used after salt. Pepper was used in preparing meat and fish, stews, soups, and sauces. It was often combined with cinnamon, cloves, nutmeg, and ginger in cookies, gingerbread, and spiced wine. At the time, techniques of food storage were primitive at best, and pepper was a preservative that was used to disguise the flavors of rotting food. Pepper was used in medicines, too, as many believed it helped with digestion. The twelfth-century German nun Hildegard von Bingen baked peppery cakes to treat nausea.

Black pepper, native to Java and cultivated along the southwestern coast of India, numbered among the most precious spices. The long distances over which it had to be carried made it extremely expensive. Peppercorns were valued equal to their own weight in gold, and medieval rulers exchanged them as gifts. Marco Polo emphasized the wealth of a certain Chinese city by declaring that "for one shipload of pepper that goes to Alexandria [in Egypt] or elsewhere to be taken to Christian lands, there are a hundred to this port of Zaitun."

The trade routes to Europe from the Spice Islands came through Egypt, via the Red Sea and the Nile, and then across the Mediterranean Sea to Venice. The disruption to European trade caused by the Crusades was made worse in 1429, when the Egyptian sultan declared a monopoly on the spice trade. The Venetian merchants, who imported 2,500 tons (2,267,961.8 kg) of pepper and ginger a year in the fifteenth century, were particularly hard hit by the royal monopoly. It was this threat that stimulated the European search for direct sea routes to India and the East Indies.

build. It had a flat bottom so it could be beached for loading and unloading cargo.

In the fourteenth and fifteenth centuries, the hulk replaced the cog in northern Europe. Hulks were broad and rounded, with high bows and sterns. They were extremely strong and held a great deal of cargo.

In the fifteenth century, Portuguese shipbuilders combined elements of these northern designs with features of Mediterranean ships. The result was the fast, oceangoing ship that ushered in the age of discovery: the caravel. At the same time, navigational aids improved dramatically. Starting in the late twelfth century, European sailors began to use magnetic compasses, allowing them to locate directions. (Such compasses had been available to Chinese navigators since about the ninth century.) Early magnetized compass needles simply floated in bowls of water. By the fifteenth century, they were mounted on cards marked with the directions. The magnetic compass had a northerly orientation. This led to maps being drawn with north at the top.

Two other important instruments were the astrolabe and the quadrant, which were used to determine latitude. They, too, became available in the fifteenth century. By the late Middle Ages, accurate hourglasses allowed sailors to measure time precisely. This helped improve the accuracy of dead reckoning, a traditional method of navigation then still in use. Accurate time measurements also led to a new measure of nautical distance, the league. One league equaled the distance an average ship could sail in one hour in good conditions.

In the centuries to come, the great European voyages of discovery produced wealth, settlement, and colonization. Why the Europeans? There is no simple answer to this question. For one thing, Europeans had a strong incentive to seek distant parts. From the time of their conversion to Christianity, they had been drawn to the East. No other advanced civilization seemed interested in exploration.

Another incentive was trade. European merchants had long-standing contacts in the Middle East. Venetian merchants were permanently established along the Black Sea by the thirteenth century. Europeans wanted more and more exotic goods. To supply them, traders looked for direct access to the spices and luxuries of the Far East and the gold of Africa. Europeans were eager to profit from trading directly at the source of these goods, and they sought sea routes to the East Indies in the late Middle Ages. The tremendous program of Portuguese exploration in the

An astrolabe from the fourteenth century is shown above. Its many uses include determining latitude and predicting the positions of the Sun, the Moon, planets, and stars.

fourteenth and fifteenth centuries aimed specifically to discover these routes. The Atlantic also attracted Europeans. As the Middle Ages drew to a close, it seemed more and more likely that Asia lay on the other side.

The Middle Ages are the rich background of the European age of discovery. The great explorers who reached and explored the Americas, discovered the long sea routes to India, and circumnavigated the globe did not spring from some dark age. They were instead the beneficiaries of hundreds of years of smaller discoveries. These smaller discoveries were made by generations of earlier sailors, shipbuilders, navigators, scholars, mapmakers, and ordinary travelers—not only European, but Muslim, Indian, and Chinese as well.

Chronology

ca. 1500 B.C.	Hindu scriptures from India, the Vedic texts, describe pilgrimages to thousands of sacred rivers, mountains, and other sites.
A.D. 105	Chinese invent paper.
Third century A.D.	Chinese invent the magnetic compass. It is used for navigation by the Chinese in the ninth century.
A.D. 399	First known Chinese Buddhist pilgrim, Faxian, travels overland from eastern China to India.

Timeline

Third century A.D.
Chinese invent the magnetic compass. It is used for navigation by the eleventh century

A.D. 500–800
The spread of Buddhism, Christianity, and Islam inspire the first wave of long-distance pilgrimages across Europe and Asia

ca. 1500 BC

1000

ca. 1500 B.C.
The Vedic texts describe pilgrimages to thousands of sacred rivers, mountains, and other sites

A.D. 610
Prophet Muhammad founds Islam, uniting peoples from the western Mediterranean to northwestern India

ca. 1000
Leif Ericsson explores the coast of North America

Fourth century A.D.	Buddhist missionaries travel from India to China.
A.D. **500–800**	The spread of Buddhism, Christianity, and Islam inspire the first wave of long-distance pilgrimages across Europe and Asia.
Sixth century A.D.	Indian mathematicians create Arabic numerals, allowing Indian sailors to navigate in open seas a thousand years before western European sailors.
A.D. **550**	Varahamihira discovers the number zero.
A.D. **610**	Prophet Muhammad founds Islam. It spreads rapidly, uniting peoples from the western Mediterranean to northwestern India.
Eighth century A.D.	Chinese invent printing with blocks.

1271–1295
Marco Polo travels extensively throughout the Chinese empire, a region few Europeans had ever heard of or visited

1325–1353
Ibn Battutah travels 75,000 miles over about 30 years

1431–1433
On his seventh voyage, Zheng He's fleet sails 12,600 miles

1251

1434

1251–1294
Grandsons of Genghis Khan rule over the largest empire in the world, reaching from the China Sea to Mediterranean Sea

1405–1422
Zheng He's first six voyages establish a Chinese presence and impose imperial control over trade in the Indian Ocean

1434
Gil Eannes becomes first to discover a passable route around Cape Bojador. This marks the beginning of inland Portuguese exploration in Africa

A.D. 732	Buddhist monk develops the first mechanical clock. In 1090 Astronomer Su Sung creates a more dependable timepiece.
A.D. 812	Chinese government begins printing paper currency.
A.D. 840	Viking settlers found the city of Dublin in Ireland.
A.D. 866	Danish Vikings establish a kingdom in York, England.
A.D. 911	Viking chief Rollo founds Normandy in France.
A.D. 981	Erik the Red discovers Greenland.
A.D. ca. 1000	Leif Ericsson explores the coast of North America.
ca. 1200	The first sagas, Norse heroic stories, are written down after centuries of oral storytelling.
1251–1294	Mangu Khan (1251–1259) and Kublai Khan (1260–1294), grandsons of Genghis Khan, rule over the largest empire in the world, reaching from the China Sea to Mediterranean Sea.
1271–1295	Marco Polo travels extensively throughout the Chinese empire, a region few Europeans had ever heard of or visited. His book about his travels, *Description of the World*, or *Travels*, makes him famous.
1325–1353	Ibn Battutah travels 75,000 miles (120,701 km) over about 30 years. He writes a travel narrative called *A Gift to the Observers Concerning the Curiosities of the Cities and the Marvels Encountered in Travels*, commonly referred to as Battutah's *Rihla*.
Early 1380s	Civil servant and diplomat, Geoffrey Chaucer, writes the *Canterbury Tales*, a group of stories told by pilgrims traveling on foot from London to Canterbury, England.
1405–1422	Chinese emperor Yongle sponsors Zheng He's first six voyages to establish a Chinese

	presence and impose imperial control over trade in the Indian Ocean.
1431–1433	On his seventh voyage, Zheng He visits Champa (present-day Vietnam), Java, Sumatra, Malacca (on the Malay Peninsula), Ceylon (Sri Lanka), and the Indian seaport of Calicut. Zheng's fleet sails 12,600 miles (20,277.7 km).
1434	Gil Eannes becomes the first to discover a passable route around Cape Bojador, on the northern coast of the western Sahara. This marks the beginning of inland Portuguese exploration in Africa.

Glossary

armada—A fleet of ships, usually heavily-armed warships, sailing together.

astrolabe—A navigational instrument that shows the position and altitude of the sun and the stars. It consists of a disk with a sighting tube. Improvements to astrolabes in the fifteenth century allowed mariners to determine their latitude more accurately.

caravan—A group of travelers journeying together for safety. Usually it refers more specifically to a group of traders traveling through a desert on camels, particularly in Asia or Africa.

caravel—A small ship developed by the Portuguese in the fourteenth and fifteenth centuries for oceangoing voyages. Combining elements of European and Arab ships and of shallow draft, they were extremely fast and responsive to changes in the direction and strength of the wind.

cartography—The science or skill of making maps. During the Middle Ages, cartographers (mapmakers) made accurate maps of increasingly large regions of the world as explorers and other travelers supplied them with firsthand geographical information.

clinker-built—Describing ships' hulls, or bodies, built from overlapping planks, nailed or strongly tied together, and then filled in with a supporting frame. See also carvel-built.

cog—A sailing ship with its straight bow (front) and stern (back) sharply angled upward; it had a flat bottom, making it easier to unload cargo in shallow tidal areas.

coracle—A small, round boat made of woven wicker covered with animal hides. Irish monks used them on their solitary voyages around the British Isles in the early Middle Ages.

curragh—From *currach* in the Celtic language, a larger coracle used in Ireland.

dead reckoning—A simple method of navigation at sea in which a voyage is broken down into segments, each of a known direction and a specific length of time.

draft—The minimum depth of water needed to float a given boat or ship.

dugout—A simple canoe made by hollowing out a log or the trunk of a tree.

Far East—Eastern and southeastern Asia, as regarded collectively from a European point of view. For the Middle Ages, this term refers primarily to China and the territory occupied by the Mongols.

ghoul—In legends and myths, an evil spirit. For Muslims, ghouls referred specifically to those who ate the dead in graves.

hajj—The pilgrimage to Mecca that all Muslims are required by Islamic law to make once in their lifetime.

Holy Land—Jerusalem and the surrounding region, which includes numerous sites connected with the life and ministry of Jesus Christ and incidents related in the Bible.

hostel—An inexpensive lodging that provides basic accommodations for travelers.

hulk—A large, broad ship, usually with a single mast, developed in northern Europe in the fourteenth century. Their rounded shape made hulks slow but gave them a large cargo capacity.

junk—A strong, oceangoing ship developed in China. Extremely stable with a flat bottom, multiple masts and sails, and a large sternpost rudder (mounted on the back end), junks were the most advanced ships in the medieval world.

keel—The long structural piece of a ship that extends along the center line of the bottom, between the bow (front end) and the stern (back end).

knarr—A broad, heavy ship with a single sail, used by the Vikings in the open seas. Knarrs were partly covered by decks to protect the passengers, livestock, and cargo.

longship—(longboat) A long, light ship with high prows (projections at the front). Used by the Vikings, they were among the most treasured possessions of the Norse warriors, who were often buried or cremated in them.

magnetic compass—A navigational instrument that contains a magnetized needle that points to the North Magnetic Pole, the region near the North Pole where Earth's magnetism is most intense.

mandate—An official instruction or order from some higher authority.

mappa mundi—A type of large, round map of the world made in Europe in the twelfth and thirteenth centuries that represented a Christian point of view. *Mappae mundi* (plural) emphasized important Christian cities and sites and often ignored others, but they sometimes incorporated recent geographical discoveries.

monsoon—A wind system that reverses direction seasonally. In the Indian Ocean, from April to September, the wind blows constantly from west to east and then reverses for the next six months.

pilot—A sea officer who is experienced and practiced in particular waters and is therefore engaged to guide unfamiliar ships in or through dangerous passages.

planisphere—A map representing the world as a sphere on a flat surface.

Pole Star—(North Star) The star Polaris, a very bright star in the northern constellation the Little Dipper. From any vantage point, it indicates due north, so it has been an important guide for navigators for thousands of years.

portolan—A chart of the seacoast accurately showing the outline of coastlines and harbors, landmarks, cities, and compass directions.

quadrant—A navigational instrument that shows the altitude of the sun and the stars. It consists of a wood or metal quarter-circle, its curved side marked with degrees, and a plumb line. Quadrants were used by mariners from the fifteenth century onward to determine latitude.

rihla—An Arabic book recounting a religious pilgrimage or other travels.

saga—A long prose story of heroes and their deeds. Norse sagas were handed down orally for centuries before being written down. They contain a great deal of information about the Norse exploration and settlement of the North Atlantic.

sternpost rudder—A rudder, or blade for steering, that is mounted on the stern, or rear, of a ship. It gives better control than a rudder mounted on the side.

stupa—A Buddhist shrine or temple, often containing a sacred relic.

tribute—Money or other valuables paid by one ruler to another, stronger ruler or by a person or group to someone who has authority over them.

Bibliography

Adler, Elkan Nathan. *Jewish Travelers in the Middle Ages: 19 Firsthand Accounts.* New York: Dover, 1987.

Boorstin, Daniel J. *The Discoverers.* New York: Random House, 1985.

Brock, Timothy. *The Confusions of Pleasure: Commerce and Culture in Ming China.* Berkeley: University of California Press, 1998.

Burgess, Glyn S., and W. R. J. Barron. *The Voyage of St. Brendan: Themes and Variations.* Exeter, U.K.: University of Exeter Press, 2002.

Carpini, John Plano. *The Story of the Mongols We Call the Tartars.* Trans. Erik Hildinger. Wellesley, Mass.: Branden Publications, 1996.

Christiansen, Eric. *The Norsemen in the Viking Age.* Oxford: Blackwell, 2000.

Dunn, Ross. *The Adventures of Ibn Battuta: A Muslim Traveler of the Fourteenth Century.* Berkeley: University of California Press, 1989.

Fernández-Armesto, Felipe. *Before Columbus: Exploration and Colonization from the Mediterranean to the Atlantic, 1229–1492.* Philadelphia: University of Pennsylvania Press, 1992.

Hamdun, Said, and Noel King, eds. *Ibn Battuta in Black Africa.* Princeton, N.J.: Markus Wiener, 1995.

Hourani, George F. *Arab Seafaring in the Indian Ocean in Ancient and Early Medieval Times.* Princeton, N.J.: Princeton University Press, 1995.

Ingstad, Helge, and Anne Stine Ingstad. *The Viking Discovery of America: The Excavation of a Norse Settlement in L'Anse aux Meadows, Newfoundland.* New York: Facts On File, 2001.

Larner, John. *Marco Polo and the Discovery of the World.* New Haven, Conn.: Yale University Press, 1999.

Levanon, Yosef. *The Jewish Travelers of the Twelfth Century.* Lanham, Md.: University Press of America, 1980.

Levathes, Louise. *When China Ruled the Seas: The Treasure Fleet of the Dragon Throne, 1405–1433.* New York: Simon & Schuster, 1994.

Maalouf, Amin, and Jon Rothschild. *The Crusaders Through Arab Eyes.* New York: Schocken Books, 1989.

Mas'udi, al-. *The Meadows of Gold: The Abbasids.* Ed. Paul Lunde. Trans. Caroline Stone. London: Kegan Paul, 1989.

Menzies, Gavin. *1421: The Year China Discovered America.* New York: William Morrow, 2003.

Odoric of Pordenone. *The Travels of Friar Odoric: Fourteenth Century Journal of the Blessed Odoric of Pordenone.* Trans. Sir Henry Yule. Grand Rapids, Mich.: William Eerdmans, 2001.

Russell, Peter E. *Prince Henry "the Navigator": A Life.* New Haven, Conn.: Yale University Press, 2001.

Severin, Tim. *The Brendan Voyage.* New York: Modern Library, 2000.

Silverberg, Robert. *The Realm of Prester John.* Columbus: University of Ohio Press, 1996.

Stetoff, Rebecca. *Vasco da Gama and the Portuguese Explorers.* New York: Chelsea House, 1993.

Webb, Diana. *Medieval European Pilgrimages, c.700–c.1500.* New York: Palgrave Macmillan, 2002.

———. *Pilgrims and Pilgrimages in the Medieval West.* London and New York: I. B. Tauris, 2001.

Whitfield, Susan. *Life Along the Silk Road.* Berkeley: University of California Press, 2001.

William of Rubruck. *The Mission of Friar William of Rubruck.* Ed. Peter Jackson. London: Hakluyt Society, 1990.

Further Resources

Ali, Tariq. *The Book of Saladin: A Novel.* New York: Verso Books, 1999.

Andrews, John. *A Viking Daughter.* New York: Doubleday, 1989.

Arsand, Daniel. *The Land of Darkness.* Trans. Christine Donougher. Gardena, Calif.: Dedalus, 2001.

Backburn, Julia. *The Leper's Companion.* New York: Pantheon Books, 1999.

Bernstein, Richard. *Ultimate Journey: Retracing the Path of an Ancient Buddhist Monk Who Crossed Asia in Search of Enlightenment.* New York: Vintage, 2002.

Chaucer, Geoffrey. *The Canterbury Tales.* Trans. Nevill Coghill. New York: Penguin Books, 2003.

Griffiths, Paul. *Myself and Marco Polo: A Novel of Changes.* New York: Random House, 1989.

Jennings, Gary. *Journeying.* Cutchogue, N.Y.: Buccaneer Books, 1998.

MacDonald, Fiona. *The World in the Time of Marco Polo.* New York: Dillon Publishing, 1997.

Ohler, Norbert. *The Medieval Traveller.* Trans. Caroline Hillier. Woodbridge, U.K.: Boydell & Brewer, 2000.

Tsiang, Hiuen. *Si-Yu-Ki: Buddhist Records of the Western World.* Trans. Samuel Beal. London: Taylor & Francis, 2000.

Vollmann, William T. *The Ice Shirt.* New York: Viking, 1990.

VHS/DVD

Biography: Marco Polo (2000). A&E Entertainment, VHS, 2000.

The Crusades (1995). 4 vols. A&E Entertainment, VHS, 1997.

Hajj 2001—A Journey of Faith (2000). CNN Video, VHS, 2000.

History's Mysteries—The True Story of Marco Polo (2000) A&E Home Video, VHS, 2000.

Islam—Empire of Faith (2001). PBS Home Video, DVD, 2001.

The Message (1976). Anchor Bay Entertainment, VHS/DVD, 1998.

NOVA—The Vikings (2000). PBS Video, VHS, 2001.

Secret Heart of Asia: Buddha on the Silk Road (1998). Mystic Fire, VHS, 1998.

Secrets of the Dead: The Lost Vikings (2000). PBS Home Video, VHS, 2000.

The Silk Road (1991). 12 vols. Central Park Media, VHS, 1991–92.

The Thirteenth Warrior (1999). Touchstone, VHS/DVD, 2002.

Viking Explorers (2000). A&E Entertainment, VHS, 2000.

The Vikings (1958). MGM, VHS, 1991, DVD, 2002.
Viking Voyages (2000). Discovery Channel, VHS, 2000.
Vikings in America (1995). WGBH Video, VHS, 2000.

WEB SITES

Fordham University: "Medieval Texts in Translation"
http://www.fordham.edu/halsall/sbook2.html
Full texts of reference sources for Medieval Studies.

Foster, Margaret A.: "The Crusades"
http://www.medievalcrusades.com
This site is a comprehensive source for information about the Medieval Crusades. It includes reviews of television and film about the Middle Ages, book reviews, maps, bibliography, and links to other sites about medieval history.

India Travelogue: Pilgrim Places
http://www.indiatravelogue.com/leis/pilg/pilg10.html
Facts about India, Buddhist sites, a photo gallery, and travel reports.

Mariners' Museum: Age of Exploration
http://www.mariner.org/educationalad/ageofex/
The online resource for the largest international maritime history museum. Includes information on exploration in ancient times up to Captain Cook's voyage to the Pacific, photographs, and resources for students and teachers.

National Geographic Society: "Marco Polo"
http://ngm.nationalgeographic.com/ngm/0105/feature1/index.html
A three-part article about Marco Polo written by a journalist who traveled in his footsteps.

PBS, NOVA: "The Vikings"
http://www.pbs.org/wgbh/nova/vikings
The companion Web site to "The Vikings," a two-hour program that examines the lives of the Norsemen based on archaeological findings.

PBS, NOVA: "Ancient Chinese Explorers"
http://www.pbs.org/wgbh/nova/sultan/explorers2.html
Maps, photographs, and text examining ancient Chinese exploration, including explorer Zheng He.

San Francisco Unified School District: "Ibn Battuta"
http://www.sfusd.k12.ca.us/schwww/sch618/Ibn_Battuta/Ibn_Battuta_Rihla.html
A virtual tour of the life of fourteenth century explorer Ibn Battuta. Includes student activities and teacher notes.

Picture Credits

Index

Names beginning with al- are listed under the second element of the name.

About the Contributors

Author **PAMELA WHITE** holds a B.A. from Carleton College and an M.A. from Princeton University in English literature. She also received an M.B.A. from the University of Massachusetts at Amherst. White has worked as an editor and freelance writer for more than a decade. She has taught writing and humanities at the University of Massachusetts and has worked as a lexicographer for Encarta. White is the author and contributing writer to more than a dozen books and articles.

General editor **JOHN S. BOWMAN** received a B.A. in English literature from Harvard University and matriculated at Trinity College, Cambridge University, as Harvard's Fiske Scholar and at the University of Munich. Bowman has worked as an editor and as a freelance writer for more than 40 years. He has edited numerous works of history, as well as served as general editor of Chelsea House's AMERICA AT WAR set. Bowman is the author of more than 10 books, including a volume in this series, *Exploration in the World of the Ancients, Revised Edition.*

General editor **MAURICE ISSERMAN** holds a B.A. in history from Reed College and an M.A. and Ph.D. in history from the University of Rochester. He is a professor of history at Hamilton College, specializing in twentieth-century U.S. history and the history of exploration. Isserman was a Fulbright distinguished lecturer at Moscow State University. He is the author of 12 books.